THE **CRITICAL PILLARS** OF MAKING **QUALITY CONTACTS** AND **CONNECTIONS**

i

THE CRITICAL PILLARS
OF CONTACTS
AND CONNECTIONS

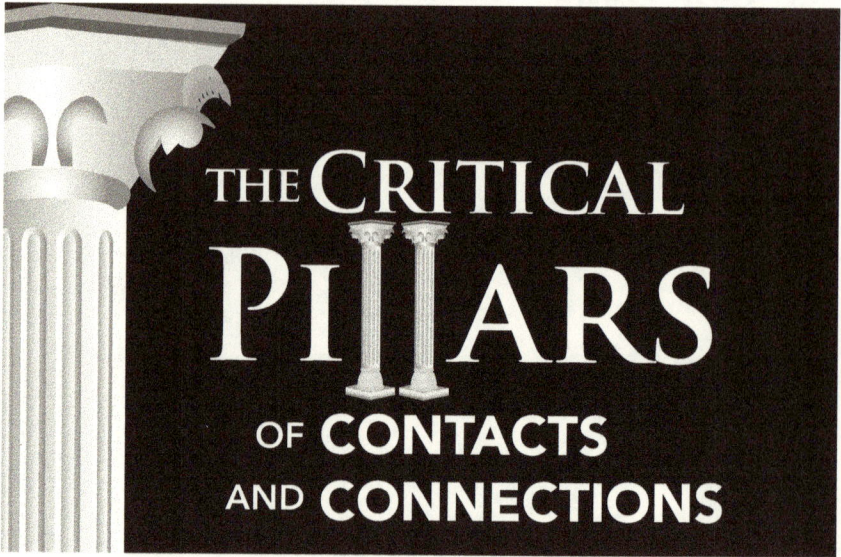

How to meet people, manage contacts,
build and develop relationships for business
and career success

FERDINAND M.
IBEZIM

Selling Skills Support Services Limited

Published by Selling Skills Support Services Limited.

Email: info@sellingskillsng.com

me@ferdinandibezim.com

Telephone: +234 807 800 0000

+234 809 999 9340

Website: www.ferdinandibezim.com

www.sellingskillsng.com

Cover & Interior Design:

Efphatha CCS: 0809 866 8480

ISBN - 978-978-962-033-3

TABLE OF CONTENT

Dedication

This book is dedicated to the most important contacts and connections in my life:

Lord God Almighty – the source of life, wisdom and grace.

My family – the source of love, joy and laughter.

Introduction

Business has always relied on effective interaction between people to generate opportunities. People acquire a vast amount of their success, breakthroughs, knowledge and resources through other people. Unfortunately, even professionals whose careers and business results are completely dependent on meeting people, managing contacts and building relationships do not seem to appreciate the importance of these critical skills.

You have probably heard stories of men and women, young and old that met complete strangers in the aircraft, buses, churches, mosques, neighborhoods, conferences, parties etc. who opened up to these strangers, introduced themselves, started a conversation; subsequently developed a relationship, managed the contacts and had their lives, businesses, careers, income, etc. turned around for good. It can be that simple. But the key word here is MET! They met the strangers. There was a contact. There was a connection.

Sometimes, these are meetings between lowly placed people and highly influential people. At other times, it can be a meeting between someone who needed information and another person that had information, between someone who needed help and one who had help; between one who needed direction and one who knew the way. There was a contact. There was a meeting. A contact, a meeting with the potentials to change lives.

Talent alone will not save you in today's economy. Oh talent is good and important, but there are many talented musicians wasting in the streets today; there are many footballers talented and good enough to play in the biggest clubs in the world, who are wasting in bad pitches across the country; there are many talented painters, fashion designers, etc. who are living in penury. These people have no challenge with talent. They have a big issue with contacts. They have a big issue with the quality of their contacts.

Tuface Idibia, the African Queen Superstar crooner, is not the most talented artiste in Nigeria. Neither is the P-Square duo, D-banj or even 9ice. The most talented artistes are found playing in local bars, they're in the villages, in churches, singing with wonderful voices, but they need more than their talent to become superstars.

Without attempting to detract the hard work and talent of Tuface, I dare say that he would not have become the superstar he is today if he had not met the duo of Di and Kenny, and been signed on by Kennis Music. He probably would not have been as big as he is today. All those great talents in the local bars singing *"ayaga-yaga-yaga-yo"* will need someone like Kennis Music, Malvin Records, etc. to take them from being local superstars to becoming international superstars.

There are so many talented footballers that are wasting in the rural areas. Austin "Jay-Jay" Okocha, the former captain of the Nigerian senior team, was a talented midfielder! But, even in his hey days, he was not the most talented midfielder in Nigeria. There were many other talented midfielders playing in local fields in the villages. Nobody discovered them. They had the talent but it was not sufficient to bring them out of obscurity. Oh yes, talent will make room for a man, but you need more than talent to survive.

The traditional advice to get more training and education is fantastic, but insufficient on its own to launch you. Your education and qualifications will not necessarily guarantee you a good job. Of course, I encourage you to get a good education and obtain good qualifications. But I am sure that there were classmates of yours who were head and shoulders more intelligent than you, who made better grades, who have MBAs from the best universities in the world but who are earning peanuts. The problem is not with their education, qualification or competence. The problem is with the quality of their contacts.

Your product, price, promotion and place will not on their own guarantee you good sales. You know why? For every product of your company, other companies have similar products - only with a different name. Other companies can give as much discount as you; can make as much noise by way of jingles and adverts as you do; can open as many branches as your company. If you are a sales person, your figures will be a reflection of the number and quality of the contacts that you have.

You need quality contacts. You need a good network.

The government will not save you. No matter how good a government is with policies and programs, you will still find poor people. And no matter how bad a government is, you will still find people who are doing very well. Sure, it's critical that government provides the enabling environment for us to prosper. However, you need more than your talent, you need more than your education, you need more than your product and you need more than your the government to save you.

I strongly believe that we should all be passionate about building business and social networks – vertical and horizontal. Of course, the more powerful your network, the more primed you are to maximizing your potentials and achieving your aspirations in life. I strongly believe that the quality of your life cannot be greater than the quality of your contacts and network. If you had better contacts, your life would have been better than it is today. Your business would have been flourishing better. The value of the business you are managing today is a reflection of the quality of your contacts. Put another way, the more and better people you meet and connect with, the higher the quality of your life.

CRITICAL QUESTION: Who Do You Need To Meet?

1. Who do you need to meet to fulfill your purpose, realize your vision and achieve your goals in life?

2. Who do you need to meet to get a good job?

3. Who do you need to meet to get that contract?

4. Who do you need to meet to obtain a scholarship?

5. Who do you need to meet to get grants and donations?

6. Who do you need to meet to get a government appointment?

7. Who do you need to meet to get spiritual counsel for the burden on your soul?

8. Who do you need to meet to get medical help for your health challenges?

9. Who do you need to meet to get admission for yourself or your ward?

10. Who do you need to meet to attract amenities to your community?

11. Who do you need to meet to showcase your talent?

12. Who do you need to meet to win that election?

Who Do You Need To Meet?

Networking is about answering these questions:
- Who do you need to meet to move your life, business and career a notch higher?
- Who do you need to meet to unleash and maximize your potentials?
- Who do you need to meet to solve the problems that you cannot solve on your own and to deal with the issues you can't handle alone?

I sometimes see and think of wasted lives everywhere. I see people who have wasted or are wasting their lives, not because they don't possess the potential or talents, not because they are not determined and hardworking; but because there is no connection between their talents or potential and the people who can help them. So talent, dreams and huge potential are wasted because of the lack of the 'meet factor". They have not met the right people.

Business and social networking is the bridge between your latent talent or potential and the crystallization of the potential.

This book will offer you practical tips, techniques and step-by-step actions you can start implementing immediately to meet and connect to the right individuals and the groups that you desperately need to achieve your targets, dreams and aspirations at work, in business and in your life.

In this book we would be examining what business and social networking is, the benefits of networking, the competencies, traits and habits of successful networkers, how to plan for networking, the right places to go for networking, the tools for networking.

We shall also examine the etiquettes, subtleties and rules of networking, how to introduce yourself to strangers, how to initiate a conversation, how to sustain a conversation, how to join a conversation, how to end a conversation, how to network in different platforms, how to use social media for networking, how to manage contact information, how to manage relationships effectively, how to make the relationship symbiotic and how to convert your network into a good net worth. This is a practical, how-to book.

PART ONE

Critical Underpinnings of Making Quality Contacts and Connections

GETTING READY FOR BUSINESS AND SOCIAL

NETWORKING

Chapter 1

What is business and social networking?

"Poverty, I realized, wasn't only a
lack of financial resources; it was
isolation from the kind of people
that could help you make
more of yourself".
– KEITH FERRAZZI

I am very passionate about this topic. I hope you are too. We live in a world of enormous possibilities; a world that has left mankind the duty of exploring it; a world that has handed you the assignment of the discovery of self, people and the environment. It's our job to daily explore the world and the people around us.

Sometimes, I ask myself, "Ferdinand, how far have you gone on your discovery assignment? Take a closer look at that man, that lady, that father, that mother, that foreigner, that clergy, that teacher, that attorney, that security man, that sportsman, that businessperson, around the corner. Have you discovered who they are? Come on, Ferdinand, time is of the essence. You better get them in your resource bank before someone else does."

What usually happens in such instances is that, while still contemplating whether to make a move or wait some more, an unassuming young man would seize the moment by stepping up boldly and taking advantage of the opportunity, while I only stare in amazement and regret. "I should have done that!" I would moan to myself in self-pity. But I wasted the opportunity by indulging in internal wrangling, instead of getting out of my shell to take advantage of the opportunity. This is the unfortunate reality of many people.

One interesting thing about networking is that anyone can start whenever he wishes. It is never too late to start. The amazing thing about the quest for opportunities is that possibilities exist both in the world and in the individual. The potentials hidden in humankind are so vast.

But only a few people have braved the odds to unlock their potential to achieve great things in life, touching the lives of other people in the process. Wouldn't you like to be around such people? Wouldn't you like to position yourself in an influential network, regardless of the age range of people in this network?

What Is Business And Social Networking?

I remember an episode that transpired one day. I had relocated to a new place, and after a meeting of the estate residents, an elderly man came to me and said he did not get my full name. I promptly obliged him. He then expressed his surprise that I was not embarrassed by his gesture, as he loved meeting people, and he encouraged me to keep doing the same.

He went on to explain that the last house he acquired was facilitated by a man he met by chance. He expressed his disappointment that some people moved into the estate and chose to isolate themselves. "Never do that anywhere you find yourself, Ferdinand." He advised. "There is a great danger in isolation. I received a call from a neighbour, some years back, who told me not to come home yet from wherever I was, as there was an armed robbery attack going on in our area at that moment. Life is so simple," he concluded. We have remained friends ever since.

Growing up in Nigeria is an interesting experience. If you turn back the hands of time and reflect on your growing up, you must have heard phrases like, "That's the son of a rich man. That's the son of a poor man. He is a friend to that rich man's son. That family is rich. Their housemaid traveled out with the family."

What category did you fall into? When you started, could you predict your life would turn out as it is today? Can you pinpoint the turnaround time? Was it because of someone you met, a contact you had, or an unexpected event that happened? In my early days, there were a number of families that I used to envy. Sometimes, I wished my family was super-rich.

I have seen people from different backgrounds rise to enviable positions in the society. Ironically, I have seen children of rich parents in those days end up in penury because they isolated themselves from people whose fortunes turned around for good over the years.

Self-isolation is a potential dream killer. Dreams that required external support and influence to be realized died because the dream promoter did not connect to destiny helpers.

Quickly move away from people who exclaim they would rather be on their own than in the company of others. Do not want to be brainwashed with such a dumb idea. Never choose to be a loner. Remember the admonition from the good book, "Woe unto him that is alone..."

I am always amazed at the turnaround of fortune for people who discovered the need to connect and network their way out of their base situation. Even some smart domestic workers who, unconsciously learnt about the need to connect, had used this simple principle to land themselves choice jobs. You surprisingly find them scouting for jobs in the highbrow areas of town, as it gives them exposure to well-heeled families.

They keep networking. You sometimes receive phone calls from them saying, *"Oga, abeg I dey find work o!* Please help me tell your friends. (Sir, I'm in dire need of a job.) Please help me tell your friends who are in need of a domestic help" When the opportunity arises, who do you think will first come to mind? These domestic workers, of course! Where you network most times reflects the possibility of where you would be tomorrow.

Moreover, beyond performing well in the entrance exams, gaining admission into tertiary institutions of choice requires some level of networking. Getting the preferred accommodation requires contact. Contact, contact, contact! That is the treasure that networking unravels. I remember visiting a friend, who lives in a very decent accommodation, and asked him how much he paid for it. I was shocked to hear a wide margin below what I paid for a similar accommodation. He simply laughed and said, *"Ferdy, na my contacts dey work"* (Ferdy, it's my contacts that made it possible).

Networking is a priority for those who desire to go the upward direction in their careers. Networking is about the most useful skill you would need to develop and connect to other upwardly mobile people as they toe the path of unveiling their potential. Those that benefit from the opportunities are those who are connected to the source. Networking keeps you connected; it keeps you in the picture and keeps you positioned for the opportunity.

Understanding Business and Social Networking

As I began my quest to become a great networker, I kept asking questions about what networking really is. Some people see it as a way to get access to people. Some view it as taking advantage of people. Others see it as a platform for information gathering. Yet, some see it as a system of building and maintaining relationships.

At this point, I would like us to define networking. It is important for us to understand concepts because they help us develop the frameworks and structures around the concepts. Having a clear understanding of the concept of networking will help you develop the strategy for putting the theories into practical actions.

It is also important for us to clearly understand the meaning of networking to serve as appraisal elements to the actions that we take in networking. In other words, if your actions don't align with the definitions I will be sharing with you, then those actions are not networking actions.

1. Networking is knocking on a door before you know what is inside the room

Networking has numerous definitions. However, in this chapter, I have captured some relevant definitions that are applicable while defining your role as a professional networker. It is important to understand the theoretical foundation of networking to ensure that what you do after now is actually networking.

A friend of mine shared a story of how he moved into a new neighbourhood; and on moving into the neighbourhood, he bought bottles of wine and went to his three immediate neighbours to introduce himself. While two of the neighbours had no qualms about his action, the third one found the action strange. This neighbour didn't understand the rationale behind someone going around to introduce himself to neighbors – stranger still with a drink in tow. So he asked my friend if he knew who he was. Of course, my friend said no; but explained to the man that it was his practice to always pay homage to those who were already leaving in a place before him. So reluctantly, this man let my friend into his house and accepted the wine. Then a conversation started.

At a point, the man asked my friend what he did for a leaving. My friend told him that he was a consultant providing training and recruitment services to organizations. Next, the man asked my friend to mention some of the clients he had worked for in the past, and my friend did. Then the man asked him if he had any clients in the oil and gas sector. My friend replied yes and listed his clients. Then he asked my friend if he was doing business with one of leading oil and gas multi nationals in Nigeria. My friend said no. He asked why and my friend said he had tried severally over the years to get a business from the company but hadn't made any head way.

To cut the long story short, right before my friend this man placed a call to the woman in charge of training in this oil company and got an appointment for my friend to meet the woman. Now, this is a woman that my friend had tried severally for years to secure an appointment with without success. Today my friend is offering training services to this company with very huge returns.

Just imagine for a moment that my friend had not gone to introduce himself to the neighbors. He could have lived close to oil field and yet had no access to the oil. Knock on the door before you know what is inside. There are several lessons from this true-life story.

The first lesson is that it is not every well that you dig that will turn out to be an oil field. But you can increase your chances of finding oil by digging more wells. It is not every neighbor you introduce yourself to that will give you a link to a business, a job or money. But you can increase your chances of finding your destiny helpers by meeting more people.

The second lesson is that you don't have to wait until you find out how people can help you before you start being nice to them. That is called parasitism. But if you are nice to people naturally as my friend was without any selfish or ulterior motive, and then an opportunity arises to help you, it will be a natural outcome of a friendly relationship.

There is something I do in my training, seminars and workshops. I usually wait till about 2.30pm for a training that started at 8.00am to move around participants asking them to introduce those sitting close to them. Amazingly, most of them would not as much as know the names of people they had sat on the same table with for over 6-7 hours. Now, remember they must have had tea breaks and lunch together, probably were in the same group for some activities; yet they will find it difficult introducing others.

But isn't that what most people do? You are traveling from Lagos to China (about 18 hours flight) or to New York (about 13 hours flight) or to London (about 7 hours flight) or even Lagos to Abuja (about 1 hour flight). What do you do? You take your seat, buckle your seat belt, have the free meal, including free red wine, read newspapers, watch movies and sleep; completely oblivious of the person sitting close to you. Meanwhile, it is possible that the person sitting by your right or your left holds the key to your future.

You go to the church or the mosque and the priest, pastor or imam says to you "Turn to the person by your left and say to him, it shall be well with you this week." Some people don't as much as look at the faces of the people they are exchanging pleasantries with. Again, it is possible that the person whose face you are not looking at is the answer to your most pressing prayer point.

You leave in a lovely neighbourhood, your neighbours don't know you, and you don't know them. It can be so bad that people don't even know the names of people leaving in the same compound with them. You are not active in estate residents meetings.

You mind your businesses too much. *You know what, if you mind your business too much, before long you would have no business to mind.* No wonder the good books says that woe unto him/her that is alone for when he/she falls there will no one to bring him/her up. Do you know what woe means? Woe means cursed, shame, reproach etc.

Some years ago, an international agency invited me to give a talk to selected entrepreneurs from different parts of West Africa and I was told to speak for two hours on business and social networking skills. About three months after the programme, my phone rang and I would like to relay verbatim my exchange with the person that called me:

"Hello, good afternoon, this is Ferdinand."

"Of course, I know it's Ferdinand. Am I not the one that called you?"

"Sorry, Sir. How may I help you?" I replied.

"My name is Peter."

"Peter who?" I enquired.

"My name is Peter ... I was one of those that attended that seminar at Ikoyi where you spoke on business and social networking skills and I have a testimony to share with you. After the training that day, I took a motorcycle from Ikoyi to Obalende where I boarded a bus going to Iyana-Ipaja, where I stay. About four bus-stops to mine, I remembered what you told us."

(I had told them that wherever they found themselves, they should introduce themselves to the people around them. I had also advised that if the environment is conducive, give your business cards to the people around you. Tell them who you are, what you do, what solutions you.)

"So, I brought out my call-card inside the bus and started introducing myself", he went on. 'Hello, my name is Peter, I'm a printer. I said the same thing to the people around me handing out my cards. Most of the passengers were looking at me curiously thinking I'd soon stand up and start to hawk something in the bus. But two stops to my bus- stop, the man sitting to my left said, 'Young man, I want to get down.' I made way for him to pass, and then he said, 'I like what you did now. Well, I'm a clerk, an office assistant in ... (he mentioned one of the big conglomerates). We just employed a new Brand Manager who complained about the quality of work of the printers we are using, and I overheard him make a request that anybody who knows a good printer should invite him to our office. So, maybe you can come to our office on Tuesday and show him what you can do.'

"Ferdinand, on Tuesday I went to that office and there were sixteen other printers who apparently must have been invited either by their friends or relatives for the same purpose. They asked us about what we had done in the past and we all showed them our respective samples. Then they asked us to go.

"About a week later, I received a call from that company inviting me to their office. I went there and this time I met about six other printers. They gave each of us samples of their letterhead, memo, call card and some other documents, and asked us to go and design dummies and samples for their review. I submitted my designs after three days. About two weeks later, they called and said I should come with a quote for some of the items they listed. Again, I went and I submitted my quote. Ferdinand, do you know that the contact I made inside that bus was God-sent? The first job I got from this organization was worth about N7.8 million!"

What Is Business And Social Networking?

The story did not end there. A few years after this conversation, Peter called me and asked what I wanted for Christmas. I asked him how his business was doing and he told me excitedly that between the first job he did for the company and the time we were speaking, which was about four years down the line, he had done other direct jobs for them, and used them as reference to do some other jobs worth over N200 million. Can you beat that? That is the power of networking in action.

Peter had since moved from the shabby one-room apartment that he was living in the suburb of Iyana-Ipaja to his own house in the high-brow Lekki area. His life has changed. Imagine what would have happened if after boarding that bus, he just sat there, like most people would, and looked at the passing cars, moaning over his lot in life. He would have still been as poor as he was several years ago.

My friends, you need more than yourself to help yourself.

I want to share a personal experience that happened some years ago. I was traveling to Massachusetts in the United States, aboard Air France, to attend a training programme. Immediately we settled down in the aircraft, I started a conversation with the people sitting around me.

The person seated by my right and I shared some things in common, so we spoke for a very long time. When we got to Paris we had to wait for about four hours, because we were to be transferred to another flight. When I got to the counter where I was supposed to be checked into the flight heading to New York, I sat down and ordered a cup of coffee. I then sighted the person that was seating beside me in the aircraft pushing his trolley and I went to give him a hand. We had coffee together and continued our chat.

When we boarded the New York-bound flight, we were not allotted

seats on the same roll. But when we got to New York and were waiting for our luggage at the baggage centre, I went up to him and we
continued the conversation. That was when he asked me what I was
in New York for. I told him I was there for a training programme and
showed him the details of the event. Then he exclaimed, "Wow!" He
had always wanted to attend the same seminar or buy the training
materials.

He then told me he was going to spend a night in New York and then
move over to Texas to meet his family. He didn't have his business
card with him so he just wrote down his name and telephone number
on a piece of paper and just mentioned the Federal parastatal where
he worked in Nigeria.

I attended the training and also got some materials for him. About
a month later I returned to Nigeria and called him. "Hello, this is
Ferdinand. We flew together from Lagos to New York and I got some
books and materials for you from the Options Institute." He initially
asked, "What books?" But while I was trying to explain, he interjected,
"Oh, oh! Now I remember. But did I mention that to you?" I said, "Yes,
Sir. How do I send them to you?"

"I'll call my cousin in Lagos to pick them up and send them to me,"
he said. "If you give me your address, I can send them to you by cou-
rier," I volunteered. Then he gave me his address and I couriered the
books to him.

The day he received them, he called me, expressed his appreciation
and then asked, "What did you say you are into again?"

"I am a competency enrichment, personal effectiveness, leadership
development and business process improvement professional sir," I
replied.

He said, "Wow! Err... do you have programmes for the public sector?" And I chirped, "Of course, Sir!"

Then he said, "Address a proposal to the Permanent Secretary, Ministry of..."

I said, "In whose attention, Sir?" And he said, "Attention me. I'm the Permanent Secretary." I almost fainted.

You can definitely guess the end of the story. I have added and received tremendous value from the works I have done for the ministry. Beyond that, I have also used this contact to penetrate other ministries; including the ones I had been prospecting for over five years without breaking through.

Imagine what would have happened if I had boarded that aircraft and had sat down, enjoyed the free meal and drinks, read newspapers and magazines and slept throughout the journey without hobnobbing with the people around me.

REMEMBER **You need more than yourself to help yourself!**

So, networking is digging wells of relationships before you need those relationships. Networking is saying to you: every and anywhere you find yourself amongst people, introduce yourself to people, tell them who you are, tell them what you do and tell them what problems you solve. Make effort to know them better. Please note strongly that we have not said, tell them what problems you have! We are saying tell them what problems you solve.

You may never know the day and place you will need the people that you meet and connect with today. You can meet somebody in the aircraft who lives in Kano while you live in Lagos. If you initiate a conversation, exchange contacts, build and manage the relationship well, you could be surprised how that the well you dug in the aircraft will quench your thirst in five years time. So, the first definition of business and social networking is that networking is the act of knocking on doors before you know who or what is inside the door.

2. Networking is swimming with the tide

The inspiration for our second definition of networking is an idiom, "They are not afraid of the river who drift with the tide." Even if you are Michael Phelps – the renowned multi medals winning swimmer and you find yourself in the middle of an ocean, with the tide, the waves and the sea flowing and moving in one direction and you are swimming in the opposite direction, it won't be long before you drown.

Not because you can't swim, (after all, you are Michael Phelps) but because you will be struggling too hard and exerting too much energy to swim; so your muscles will begin to ache, you get tired and before long you begin to drown. However, if you are just an average swimmer and you are swimming in the same direction with the tide and the waves, all you will need to do is to paddle with your hands and legs, and the current will carry you ashore.

What point are we making? In every country, in every location, in every profession and in every city, there are people and groups who directly or indirectly determine the direction of businesses, jobs, opportunities, politics, the economy, etc. There are influence peddlers, there are consent givers, and there are information sources.

For every product or service that you offer or sell, there are places where you are more likely to find good prospects and customers. If these prospects go in one direction and you are headed in the opposite direction, you are making it very difficult for yourself.

Networking is about identifying the influence holders, consent givers, information sources, places and direction where people who need what you have and have what you want go. Business and Social Networking is about aligning yourself with them, with their direction and location. It's about making them know you, making them know what you can do, showing them the value you can offer and the value you that seek in return. As the popular saying goes "You can't look for fish in a gold mine or pan for gold in a trout stream." Networking is about swimming with the tide.

**3.
Being known is more important than knowing people**

The third definition of business and social networking is that networking is getting known by those who can help you build your career, business and life. Please pay attention to this definition. I have just posited that networking is getting known by those who can help you build your career, business and life. I have not stated that that networking is knowing those who can help you build you career, business and life.

> *It is not about the people that you know. NO! It is more about the people that know you.*

I always say that if 10% of the people that you know do know you, your life will be 100% better than it is today. What do I mean? Don't you know the president of Nigeria? Do you know why you are not a minister or a personal assistant to the President with all your qualification, intelligence, integrity and so on? It is mainly because the president does not know you at all; or even if he does, he does not know you well enough to believe that you are better than the people he has appointed ministers and aides.

Don't you know all the big men and women in your churches and mosques? How come you are not meting your target in life and work?

It is because they don't know you. Don't you know most of the billionaires in Nigeria? How come you are broke? It is because they don't know you.

You, the very talented musician, don't you know who the best producers and recording labels in the world are? How come you are still carrying your demo on the streets? It is because these producers don't know you and the quality of your work.

Remember the story of my friend who moved into a new neighborhood and went around introducing himself to his neighbors? Do you know that he could have known that his neighbor was a man of influence, but if he hadn't made the man know him, he would have remained a neighbour of a big man without being big; even though the neighbour was willing and able to make him big.

I often hear people brag about the rich men from their communities, the powerful people who live in their neighbourhoods, the influential men/women who worship in the same place with them. My question for them is always: do they know you? They need to know you. They need to know who you are. They need to know what value you bring to the table. They need to know how good you are and they need to know how they can invest in you or help you.

> *My question to you is: How many of the people that need to know you for your career, business, talent and life to improve tremendously do know you? Do they know how good you are you? Do they know you need a job? Do they know your company has a product or offers a service that they need?* **What are your plans and strategies for making them know you?**

My assignment for you today is to take up a sheet of paper and list all the people that need to know you for you to achieve your potentials in life. Then draw up a plan for getting them to know you.

Let me also add that meeting people does not mean that they know you. Please permit me to share my personal experience. I started my career as a journalist. In the early 90s, I worked in one of the then leading business magazines in Nigeria. My major responsibility was to interview top chief executives, business people, politicians and professionals. So, I had the privilege of meeting and interviewing some of the biggest names in Nigeria those days.

Usually, after the interview I requested for photographs with them and they would oblige me. Then I would enlarge and frame the pictures and hang them in my very modest apartment in Lagos. So in my little apartment those days there were framed pictures of myself with these men and women of timber and caliber. But it only offered my bragging rights amongst my friend. The pictures did not add anything to my career or life.

The only value I derived from those pictures then was using them to brag to my friends. When they entered my room, I'd say, "That's my friend!" pointing at one big shot. Now if these chaps were smart enough, I expected them to have asked me, "Ferdinand, if these guys are your friends, why are you living here?" Well, none of them asked.

Do you know why I did not benefit from those meetings? I didn't make these prominent people that I met know me. I didn't sell value. I didn't take meting them to the next level. I didn't follow up with a phone call, letters, visits or gifts. I didn't manage the contacts and relationships. I didn't enshrine myself in their consciousness.

I am sure that the quality of my life today would have been much better if I had made some of these people know me. In other words, if I had progressed from just meeting them, knowing them to making them know me.

The point is, I knew these top shots, but they did not know me. It had not become networking simply because I had not exploited the relationship. They didn't know me because they did not know what my needs were; they did not know what value I could add. After the interview I had with them, I did not nurse the relationship, so it was not networking. They were not helping me to build my career or business. It's not sufficient to just collect people's call cards in the aircraft or in the church and say, "Ah, I know that man!"

REMEMBER

Business and social networking is about getting known by those who can help you build your business, career and life.

This leads us to the fourth definition of networking; which is that business and social networking is building and nurturing long-term relationships. Again I will share a personal experience with you. One of the current state Governors in Nigeria was not only my classmate in the university; we shared the same room for two years. We were so close that during the holidays, we either went to my parents' house in Enugu or stayed in his parents' house in Port Harcourt.

**4.
It's about today, tomorrow and the future**

Back then, there was nothing about him to sign post that he will be a governor today. But I was neither the only classmate nor the only roommate he had in the university. Today however, some of his former classmates, roommates, etc. have no access to him. No, it is not because he has become a governor, nor because he is now arrogant. It is mainly because some people did not build and nurture the relationship.

You see, relationships have first lifetime value, second lifetime value and third lifetime value. The times you spent with your schoolmates in primary, secondary and university offered some level of value. That was the first lifetime value. You enjoyed each other's company, cracked jokes, played pranks, supported each other academically and perhaps emotionally and so on. For most people, the relationship ended on leaving the university or secondary school. Years later, you suddenly hear that one of your classmates is now a minister, the managing director of a big conglomerate, the head of human resources offering good jobs to people, the Personal Assistant to the President, the Governor, etc. That's when you now seek to reconnect; and if for any reason you are encumbered by protocol from seeing this old friend, you label him/her arrogant.

Now you are seeking the second lifetime value of the relationship. You know what? You do not deserve a second lifetime value unless you had nurtured the relationship at the first lifetime. Which is why joining alumni associations, keeping in touch with old friends and colleagues are part of networking. There is a time to build a relationship, there is a time to nurture a relationship and then there is the time to benefit from the relationship. If you have not planted, watered, weeded and tended you farm very well, you do not deserve a good harvest.

One of the participants to one of my trainings also shared with us how that she attended a 2-week course with a delegate from another company who at the time of writing this book is the Governor in one the northern states in Nigeria. She told us how that they shared the same table throughout the training. But after the training, they didn't keep in touch; no telephone calls, no emails, and no connection whatsoever. But today, she is desperately seeking for an opportunity and appointment to meet with this man to introduce a wonderful package she has for schools. Unfortunately for her, she did not build and she did not nurture the relationship. So she is finding very difficult to reconnect with this contact.

A lot of people are regretting today because of past relationships they neither built nor nurtured. Those who destroy relationships because of temporary disagreements do not understand the meaning of networking.

While I was doing my youth service in Warri, Delta state, an elderly man saw me talking rudely to a pregnant woman and said to me "Young man, respect all stomachs, you don't know which one will produce the next president." For me, that means build, nurture and honor all relationships. You don't know which one will save you tomorrow.

Let me also add that networking follows a process. It starts with meeting people or being introduced to people, joining a group or an association, building the relationship by adding value, demonstrating competence, proving that you are reliable and trustworthy, nurturing the relationship by selflessly depositing in the emotional account of people and being of service. You know what? I have been long enough in networking to guarantee that you will eventually benefit from these relationships directly or indirectly. The process might take one week, one month, one year, ten years or fifty years. Business and social networking is all about building and nurturing long-term relationships.

**5.
Mass and
velocity**

The fifth definition of business and social networking is that networking is the deliberate and sustained act of creating momentum towards business and career success. What is momentum? In physics, the equation for momentum is $p = mv$; where M is mass and V is velocity. In other words, momentum is mass multiplied by velocity that produces motion, speed or force.

Please pardon me if I am wrong; but I can deduce therefore that if momentum is mass and velocity that produce motion or force, we can say that networking is creating enough mass and velocity to cause acceleration, speed and motion in your business, career and life; where mass is the number of people that know you and velocity is the quality of the people.

Networking is building a large of number of quality contacts sufficient to fast track the achievement of your goals and aspirations in life. *I make bold to state that the quality of your life, business and career today is to large extent a reflection of the number and quality of the people that you know and of the people in your network.*

If your parents had a different set of network, you are mostly likely not to be where you are today.

When a salesperson comes to me to complain that he/she is not meeting sales targets, the first thing I do is to seek their permission to check their phones. If they oblige me, I go through their contacts on the phone to check the number of people on the phone book. Then, I ask them to tell me who the people on their phone contacts are, and what they do. So, I am checking number (mass) and quality (velocity) of the people in their phone. Eight out of ten times the ones who usually struggle to meet their targets are the ones who have less than 150 contacts in their phone book.

Worse still, when you dig deeper you will find such names as Taye the meat seller, Uche spare parts, Isah tailor, Vivian fish seller in their phone book. The other names are casual friends who add no real value to them. How can you meet your target with such momentum? How can you meet your target with such number and quality of people in your contact base?

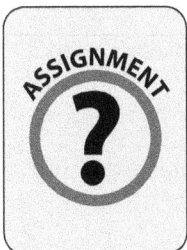

ASSIGNMENT ?

My assignment for you today is to review the number and quality of your contacts and determine the level of momentum you are generating for your business, career and life.

If you are a politician vying for an elective position, how many people do you need to know and make them know you to be able to win? What quality of people must be in your network for you to win? If you are sales person, how many prospects do you need to have to increase your chances of conversion? What quality of people do you need to meet to achieve your numbers? If you are looking for a job, who are the people you need to meet to get a job. What is your plan for meeting them?

**6.
It's a
sequence.
Make every
step count**

If you are not asking and answering these questions, you are not networking. If the people that you have around you now do not offer momentum to your business and career success, that is not a network! Networking is when you are able to galvanize and mobilize the resources, the potential, the creativity, the influence, and the power of the people around you to create velocity/motion for your life and your business.

The sixth definition is that networking is the deliberate process of meeting people, turning them into business contacts converting them to customers and then making them friends. I hope you followed the sequence. As a sales person for instance, it starts with meeting people. You can meet someone in the aircraft, gym, conference, party, and so on. Now, you are expected to introduce yourself to that person, start a conversation, get to know the person and then secure an appointment for the next meeting.

In doing this you have converted a total stranger into a contact; meaning that you can reach and keep in touch with that person because you now have the contact details. Subsequently, you are expected to convert this contact to a customer by communicating the features, benefits and competitive advantages of your products or services and persuading that person to buy.

Please permit me to digress a bit and ask every sales person reading this book some questions. How many of the people that you met in the past one month did you convert to contacts by initiating a conversation and getting their contact details? How many of the people you collected their contact details did you follow up with and have you kept in touch with? How many of the contacts did you turn to customers?

However, the above activities are merely sales activities. They don't amount to networking yet. Your customers are not necessarily in your network unless you bring them in. How many of your current customers will still be in touch with you if you lose your job or if you resign? Your company offers you a very rare platform to meet people. But it is your responsibility to convert your customers to your friends and bring them into your network.

If you leave your current place of work and set up a laundry and dry cleaning business for instance, how many of the customers you won for the company or that you serviced in the company will start patronizing you because of you and because of the relationship you have with them?

I see so many professionals, especially sales persons and customer service professionals in banks and other companies, who in the course of their careers would have met one on one with thousands of people, but when they set up their own business, they struggle with getting customers. You know why? They did not convert the customers of the bank to their friends. There is a big difference between "This person is my customer." and this customer is my friend." Did you get that? There is a big difference between "This person is my customer." and "This customer is my friend."

How many of your customers are you on first name basis with? How many of them know your personal situations? How many of them know other competencies that you have outside of the role you play in your company? How many of them have introduced you to their family members? How many have referred you to other prospects? How many of them are your advocates? How many of them will still keep in touch with you in the next ten years even if you quit your current job?

If you are not converting business platforms into friendship and network creating platforms, you are losing value. You are not networking.

The seventh definition is that networking is building a people resource bank that compounds and yields dividends for as long as you live. We all understand the principle of compound interest. Compound interest is not 1+1=2, 2+2=4, 3+3=6. No, that is simple interest. Compound interest is 2x1=2, 2x2=4, 4x4=16, 16x16=256, etc. How does that relate to networking?

Let's assume that you invite me for a party in your house and as I am coming to honor your invitation, I come with two other people who are not your friends. So I am your friend, but the other two people I come with are your friend's friends.

Typically what most people would do is to practically ignore my friends and focus on me alone. At best they would just exchange pleasantries, offer them drinks and food; and that's all.

But if you understand the principle of networking, you would actually pay more attention to my friends than me. You know why? You already have me in your network. These are the new contacts you want create and eventually bring into your network. So, what should you do? You should introduce yourself to them, initiate a conversation, establish a rapport and exchange contact details. Then after the party you either call them or send a nice text message thanking them for coming to your party. You begin to keep in touch.

What has happened? From me you have made two new friends. Now, assuming again that six months down the line you are having another event. You will invite these friends of mine individually and directly without recourse to me. Assuming again that each of us also honor your invitation with two people respectively. And you repeat the process. What has happened? You now have six new friends. If you add that to the initial three, you would have increased your contact base to nine people. Just from one person, me.

If you continue building your contact this way, you would eventually get to the point where you virtually know someone who knows someone that knows someone that has what you need and needs what you have.

So if you need medical advice for instance, you have a large pool people to get advice from. If you need direction in your business, you have a large pool of contacts that have relevant experience to draw from, and so on.

If you are sales person, your prospect list will be so long and your sales funnel always flowing with possible buyers. This is what makes the sales process easy. This is how to create a large pool of contacts that you can offer value to. And you know that your income is directly proportional to the number and quality of people that depend on you for value.

> My question to you is: How many of your friend's friends are your friends? How many of your current customers' friends are in your contact base? How many of your relatives' friends are your friends? How many of your neighbors' friends and relatives are your friends?

If you are not compounding your relationships, you are not fully maximizing the potentials and benefits of business and social networking.

I often talk about the need to create a network of people of influence around oneself. Money, they say, is a defense.

8. Networking is about creating a web of defense

However, you may not have the cash to defend yourself, but if you have people who have the cash or are influential in your network, when an embarrassing situation shows up, those people would be your defense.

The help you need is often a phone call away. With this in mind, check your network; assess the people in your phonebook and database. How strong is your defense?

I have a friend who is not particularly rich, in the sense of the word. But, in his phonebook, he has extensive contacts in the military, Police, Federal Road Safety Corps and Lagos State Traffic Management Authority. He maintains those contacts, calls them, and sends them text messages just to maintain the contact and be in their mind. He often tells me, "Ferdinand, do not disconnect, do not break the link; keep it, maintain it, value it, it can be a lifesaver."

These words are true. We must learn to act. Some people love learning the hard way. It is better to be prepared and nothing happens than for something to happen and you are not prepared.

REMEMBER

In Creativity Café, "Strangers are just friends who haven't yet met!"
– Peter Rosen

Chapter 2

The misconceptions about networking

"It's the people we hardly know,
and not our closest friends,
who will improve our lives
dramatically".
– MEG JAY

Now that we have a good understanding of the meaning of business and networking, let us now turn our focus on the misconceptions that people have about business and social networking. There are so many misconceptions that people have about networking. Let's address some of them.

1. **Networking is manipulative.** The first misconception is that networking is manipulative. Well, I agree with you that some people set out to network because they believe that they can manipulate their ways to success. The reality is that you cannot be parasitic or exploit others and succeed as a networker. Those who try it never build or manage long-term relationships.

    The way to avoid being manipulative - if that is your concern- is to deliberately seek ways and opportunities to give more than you receive. What you give doesn't have to be financial every time. Give of your time, give of your intellect, give of your resources and emotion.

2. **I am naturally an introvert or I don't have the gift of gab.** This is the second misconception. My position is that saying you are "naturally" an introvert can't be true. When you say you are "naturally" something what it connotes is that it came with you from birth. In other words, there is something in your gene, your blood group or your cell that has made you who you are.

    But that is not true. There is nothing in your genotype, blood group or cell that has predisposed you to being an introvert. The reality however is that 80% of the excellent networkers that I know were neither born with excellent communications skills nor with rapport building skills. These are learnable skills. In other words, you can overcome your introversion. You can improve your communication skills relative to networking and you can improve your rapport building skills.

3. **Networking is for those looking for jobs or business.** The third misconception is that "I am comfortable where I am". Well, I thank God for your life. I am happy for you. But you know what? I have seen and heard of so many people who thought they had job security lose their jobs. I have seen people who believed their businesses would remain successful who are broke today. More importantly though is the fact that networking is not about getting a job or growing your business. Of course, these are likely outcomes of networking, but they are not the ultimate goal.

    Beyond that, your network today can save your life tomorrow or be relevant to your kids and community in the future. I consider it selfish to say that because you are comfortable today, you don't need a network. How about your community, how about your kids and relatives? How about people out there who also need you to inspire them, motivate them and support them?

4. **Networking is a waste of time.** This is the fourth misconception about networking. I have heard people say "I'd rather use my time for better things than hang around with people I don't know or care about." You know why networking is a waste of time for some people? It is because they have no networking plan. Some also have no networking goals? They work hard to network, but they hardly work. The problem is not with networking. The problem is with them.

5. **"Networking is about exchanging business cards and contact details; Once I give and collect their contact details, they are in my network".** This is the fifth misconception about networking. No sir! Networking has stages and processes. It starts with meeting people, introducing yourselves, exchange business cards and contact details, keeping in touch, developing the contact, managing the relationship, selling value and deriving value in return. The final stage is compounding the relationship. It is a

misconception to assume that everybody whose number is in your phone book is in your network.

6. **"I don't have the resources like cars, expensive clothes and accessories to network.** The sixth misconception is, I will feel intimidated when I meet people".** While it is true that your appearance is important in networking, what is even more important is your attitude, your self-belief and your enthusiasm.

It is not possible that while you are waiting to buy a big car before you start attending your alumni association meetings, the contacts you need to buy the big car are waiting for you at the alumni meetings? Is it not possible that while you are waiting to get a good job before you start attending the women's meeting in your place of worship, that the person who can link you up with a good job is actually at that meeting? Is it not possible that while you are waiting for your business to grow before you join business groups that the business groups are waiting for you to come before your business can grow?

7. **Networking is for sales people.** The seventh misconception is to think networking is the sole preserve of sales people. You have to understand that networking is not selling and selling is not networking. While business and social networking can, and indeed would aid selling, networking is not selling. Business and social networking is about building long-term relationships even if tangible things are not exchanged.

8. **"I might run into criminals or fall victim to dupes if I start networking."** This is the eight misconception about networking. I concede that this is valid apprehension. However, if you are strategic in networking, your chances of being a victim of criminals and manipulators are very slim.

Beyond that, may I ask you a question? Are there people who

die of road crashes every day in the world? Why do you still enter vehicles? Where there people who died when they went to work today? Why did you go to work? Are there people who die eating food? So, why do you eat?

I guess I know why. It is because your focus is on the benefits, not the risks. Your focus is on the millions who arrive their destinations safely and not on the hundreds who die. Networking is about what you focus on. If you focus on the benefits, you move to get the benefits. If you focus on the risks, fear keeps you from networking. What you focus on enlarges.

9.   **"If I am good in what I do people will locate me."** The ninth misconception is to think you don't have to network. I'm glad you are good at what you do, but have you asked yourself: am I really maximizing my potentials? The fact that you are making N10 million a day does not mean that you can't make ₦50 million a day.

Are their people you can inspire and coach or mentor to be successful also? This misconception is driven mainly by arrogance and selfishness. You can never be as good as your potentials can make you. You can never be as good as others can help you be.

10.   **"I am a lady, People will misinterpret my actions and think I am throwing myself at them; networking is better done by men".** This is the tenth misconception. My question to you is: If this is your concern, haven't you had men approach you even when you are minding your own business and not networking? How did you respond in such situations? Did you throw yourself at them because they asked? Weren't some of you harassed by lectures in school? Did you quit school because of sexual harassment? Of course networking has its own risks. But the risks don't take away from the value.

Chapter 3

What contacts and connections can do for you

''Motivated minds networking together can be a powerful force creating desirable outcomes. So, surround yourself with the best possible influences while you strive to bring out the best of each other in your quest for constant and never ending improvement.''
– SANDRA RENAUX

I have realized that reward is one of the motivations of man. While growing up, we were often taught that success is the reward of hard work. So, we found ourselves working so hard to achieve success. The same holds true for laziness and complacency. They too have their rewards. Most people, at some point in their lives, realise that they could have been better off if they had taken time earlier to weigh the rewards of excelling in their chosen fields. Many expected success to fall on them in their old age. But it hardly does.

The world only pays back in direct proportion to what you put in. Weak networking efforts result in a below-average network of contacts, while calculated and aggressive networking activities yield tremendous proceeds in a powerful network. I am sure we all desire the latter. Most times the rewards are beyond you, spilling over to your children and loved ones.

Most employees of organizations are often demotivated when the rewards of the job are not commensurate with the efforts expended. Surveys have often revealed that high performing establishments have a reward system in place for their workers. Ironically, most employees do not take time to consider the rewards of excelling at their work. They, thus, fail to keep in view the picture of the reward. Consequently, there is no inspiration to drive them to perform above average or do the extraordinary

Networking is a valuable skill for people across all cadres – from the security personnel to the Chief Executive Officer. I remember often being assisted by a particular security officer to get a good parking space in one of the banks in Lagos. Every time I visited the bank, he quickly stepped up with a smile and gave a helping hand. One day, he boldly walked up to me and said, "Sir, please pardon my disturbance. My son studied Accountancy and has just finished his National Youth Service. I would be happy if you can help him get a job."

I was stunned. I told him I did not have any vacancy for his son then. But I gave him my card and told him to tell his son to drop his CV at my office. He did. About two weeks later, I was with a friend who needed an accountant in a new firm he just set up. Guess who came to my mind? Of course, the son of that security man! That is the reward of networking in action.

Please note that I am not implying that it works like this all the time. But I am certain that your chances of getting a faster payoff in life will be further brightened by effective networking.

The same holds true for vision-based networking. Once you have a vivid picture of what you stand to gain if you network effectively, your attitude towards networking will be more proactive. Remember the biblical story of David who singlehandedly brought down Goliath, the giant. Before David left for the battlefront to face Goliath, he had gone around the Israelites' camp to inquire about what the rewards for killing Goliath would be. And the rewards were good enough to motivate him to go for the kill. Same way, you need to see the reward in your mind's eye. There must be a personal buy in. It has to become a personal passion.

Before I got married, I wrote down what the rewards of getting married would be. I value a productive kitchen and the sight of children running around the house. I value being responsible and having a soul mate. These are a few rewards that motivated me to seek a partner. Seeing the rewards would create the inner inspiration to pursue and acquire the resources necessary to live your dreams.

Many years ago, I wrote down the rewards of networking, and I have ever since inscribed them in my heart to serve as motivation for me whenever a networking moment arises. I clearly remember a one-liner in my list that states, 'Ferdinand, networking would take you to a place better than where you are.' So, when a networking opportunity arises, I hear a voice screaming from within me, "Ferdinand, there is a place better than where you are, bigger than where you are, greater than you. You have the chance to move ahead. Take it, take it, and take it!" I call this my networking action-booster.

In my knowledge transfer sessions, I often tell participants that they should avoid complacency in networking and must be passionate about building their networking account. Act as if your networking account is one of your bank accounts, because it truly is. Always improve your networking ability; the fatter the account, the better for you and the better the rewards.

Just as the money in your bank account pays your bills, so the quality of your network creates the opportunities that guarantee you consistent business and income. The same way you ensure your account doesn't go into debit is the same way you ensure your network account does not go dormant. You have to keep building your account. The dividends can be a lifesaver.

I realize that one key strategy for getting ahead faster in life is to leverage on your contacts and your contacts' contacts. How many people do you know? How many quality and influential people do you know? Think back to your days in school, how many of your friends do you still have in your network? I know certain alumni of a prominent institution in Nigeria that help their peers get up faster in the ladder of success.

It is amazing to find that there are people who attended that same institution but who shy away from alumni meetings. Perhaps, they do not realize the power of such networks. The rewards of active participation in that kind of association cannot be overemphasized.

There were job seekers who have become employed, while those hitherto employed have gotten better appointments. The smart networkers have expanded their networks. The thinking networker knows that such associations are needful for advancement in career and business.

It is appalling to find people meandering all year long without a single networking platform; which is meant to be a river where they fish for business, for opportunities, and for people. I agree that some people have the capacity to fish in several places, but how many do you have? I often ask participants at my seminars how many networking platforms they fish from. You may need to ask yourself that same question regularly.

I remember having lunch with a very aggressive networker one day, and he said to me, "Sir, you may find this funny, but I have three simple networking platforms from which I have always reaped massive rewards. They are receptions, lifts and fast food restaurants. I visit these places every day and I realized that a great deal of good contacts can be harvested there." I smiled. I told him how impressed I was with his smartness, because we all visit those places too but without the mindset of a savvy networker. Maybe the next time you find yourself in those places, you can think of doing some networking.

Due to my knowledge about the rewards of networking, I was able to design a special-reward marketing approach that has paid off for me. Firstly, I check out my lifestyle or major areas of my life where I require help most times. Let us consider some – medical (a doctor), legal (a lawyer), property (a real estate consultant), and bank charges (a reliable banker).

This is what I do. I create a network plan to know at least 10 experts in all these areas. I take time to meet them one-on-one. I create and sustain all the relationships. So, whenever I have a challenge in any of those fields, I am sure to get the best advice or help, at the best price - and sometimes at no price!

I know the best rates on my funds; I get advice on how to negotiate better rates and the best paying financial investments. The legal network helps me know how to handle my legal obligations. It guides me on how not to get exposed to or entangled in sensitive legal matters. The networks pay off. If I need to buy a house, then I talk to my network on real estate. I know what the industry is paying for a particular real estate; I get the best advice on when to buy or sell and how to get fantastic deals.

Sometimes, my network just shares useful information with me by virtue of my keeping in touch. I have received free newsletters that have helped me to save millions for my clients through shared information that was a guide to their business decisions.

> The question now is, "How have you categorized your networks?" Have you taken time to list your contacts? Have you segmented them across their area of operation? Can you structure your expected reward from these network groups? But, do not forget, you must be ready to give the group some value. You must establish presence.

Our actions are consciously or unconsciously driven and motivated by rewards. We are willing to make sacrifices because of the expectations of rewards. If the prize is not worth it, nobody will pay the price. Let me say upfront that networking requires that you make sacrifices; that you pay the price. Networking will place a lot of demand on you. Demand on your time, demand on your emotion, demand on your finances, demand on your relationships and demand on your patience.

What Contacts And Connections Can Do For You

I know that it is not easy to walk up to a complete stranger, especially those of status and initiate a conversation. Sometimes you will be embarrassed, at other times you may be harassed. Networking can be expensive. Joining associations or groups, dressing for the occasion, meeting your financial obligations can put pressure on your finances.

Networking can be time consuming. You may need to sacrifice your rest and sleep time. But these are essential sacrifices to make if you must make the contacts and create the connections that will help you fast track the achievement of your goals, dreams and aspirations in life.

If you focus on the price to pay, the sacrifices to make and the demands on you the tendency is very high that you will give up midway. And nobody who gives up deserves the benefits of networking. But if you identify and focus on the rewards and benefits of networking even when the challenges show up, you are willing to face them.

You will see the demand on your time, money and resources as investments and not as expenses. A networker is like the hurdles runner. He realizes that the only way to win the race is to focus on the tape, not on the hurdles. The hurdles are only ladders to the podium. Without the hurdles, there would be no race; without the race, there would be no medals. Without the price, there would be no prize.

So, the motivation is the prize. If the crown is not worth it, nobody will go to the cross. What then are the rewards, benefits and prizes of networking? Now, let us consider some of the reasons it is so important for you to acquire and use the skills of professional networkers and why it is so important for you to improve on your networking skills.

The first benefit or reward for business and social networking is that

Reward 1: Knowledge and experiences of other people

networking exposes you to the knowledge and experiences of other people. Because of networking, you are connected to people and groups with diverse backgrounds and experiences. So here you are with just a few years in your career connecting to people who have invested three quarters of their lifetime acquiring education and working in diverse places.

You can plug in and draw from those years of experience by just connecting with them. You are also able to share your own experiences with those who can benefit from them. Ideas flow freely during networking. Information is freely given during business and social networking. You are able to learn from other people's success stories and mistakes. Others are also able to learn from yours.

Networking creates a large pool of human resources you can share your ideas, your dreams, plans and aspirations with. Two good heads they say are better than one. Imagine where you have access to hundreds or thousands of good heads.

Reward 2: Massive opportunities are opened

Networking exposes you to potential opportunities. You find yourself centered in the midst of potential opportunities that would ordinarily not have come your way at this point in your life. You have the privilege of joining associations, clubs, gyms, resident associations, religious groups and so on with men and women old enough to be your parents. Peter Drucker once said that more business decisions occur over lunch and dinner than any other place, yet no MBA courses are given on the subject of business and social networking.

What Contacts And Connections Can Do For You

You are more likely to know about job and business opportunities if you have a large and robust network. Some companies do not advertise job openings and contracts. Only those who work in those companies get to know. Guess what, only those who know the people that work in those companies also get to know. It is called knowing by knowing those who know.

So you can increase your chances of knowing by increasing the number of people who know that you know. That is what network-ing is all about. There are so many companies and institutions in Nigeria and West Africa that I provide training and consultancy services for just because someone who knows me mentioned my name to the decision makers. I am of the belief that the more you grow in your careers and business the more the openings and deals you get should come from referrals and advocacy; not from blind prospecting.

Reward 3: Less hard work

The third benefit of networking is that networking is about less hard work. If you are a sales person and you have a target to meet, you have two options. One option is for you to adopt the cold call technique; which is to knock on as many doors as possible or blindly call as many people as possible, attempt to see the decision mak-ers, book appointments, make sales presentations, start following up and hope that some of them will eventually buy from you. But that's a very laborious way of prospecting and selling. That is called working hard, but hardly working.

The other option open to you as a sales person is to use the contacts of the people you know to secure appointments. In other words, you are exploiting the contacts that people have made over the years. It is called using close contacts to gain access to distant contacts. Only business and social networking offers you this platform. Networking fast tracks the sales process.

The fourth benefit of business and social networking is that networking gives you the power to leverage on other people's network. Networking unconsciously gives you the power to enter other people's network. People have networked for years and have built very powerful networks in the process. "Can you refer me to five people I can introduce my business to?" could lead to a positive answer that will spiral you into their own bank of network. Your own duty will be to maintain your relationship with such persons and build on the others in their network.

Rewards 4: Reap where you did not sow

> Please take this advice to heart: Always maintain close contact with the principal networker, give him/her feedback on the people he/she refers you to, and thank him/her for such referral. Send a thank you text. Send a thank you card. When you earn a significant reward by virtue of the contact, you can send a simple but relevant gift. This constant feedback often results in the release of more contacts to you.

Furthermore, if you understand the principle of compounding relationships, you are able to expand your own network and leverage from other people's network. Just by joining a group or association, just by introducing yourself to people, establishing a contact and building the relationship, you are now able to leverage on the contacts, networks and relationships that others have acquired over the years.

You didn't attend the same secondary school or university with me, you are not from my village, you don't leave in my estate; but just by connecting with me and managing the relationship well, you begin to meet my class and school mates, my neighbours, my relatives and my friends. You also begin to leverage on their contacts, connections and referrals. So if I have a network of successful people, women of influence, consent givers and support team, once you join my network you will be exposed to these people and inevitably expand your own network.

So, you are just 35 years old and you meet a man of 70 years; a retired top professional or public servant who had worked for 35 years; had helped hundreds of people in key positions of authority today, and has built a formidable network of people. Imagine the opportunity that meeting this person offers you!

Having him in your network offers you the opportunity to show-case yourself to people who understand what value means and who have the ability to help you achieve your aspiration in life. Networking is the strategy for business and career acceleration. My friends, you need more than yourself to save you.

The fifth reward of business and social networking is that a good network will replace the weakness of an individual with the strength of a group. Alone, I can only achieve little; but with others practically anything is possible. We are all familiar with the story of the tower of babel. Even God himself realized that in unity man, with his all limitations could do anything. You can either raise 10 million Naira to drive a charity course close to your heart by asking 10 people to each donate 1 million Naira.

Reward 5: Strength in number

You can achieve the same objective by asking 100 people to each donate 100, 000 Naira. The other option is to ask 1,000 people to make donations of 10,000 Naira each. Assuming that all the 1,000 people have the option to donate 1 million Naira, 100,000 Naira or 10,000 Naira which option do you think will help you achieve your objective faster and with fewer burdens on people?

People struggle to achieve lofty dreams and aspirations because of a limited network. Even in physical exercises, you are more likely to stretch yourself when exercising with others than when you are exercising alone. In the gym, you are more likely to lift an extra KG, run five more minutes on the thread mill because of the motivation and challenge from others.

The sixth reward of business and social networking is that the right network gives you the power to break barriers and open shut doors.

Reward 6: Break barriers and protocol

I remember sitting out with a friend who said to me, "Ferdinand, I am really shocked you are not a member of that club. How can you live your dreams? I am always passionate about your ideas but such dreams need people, need strong networks to see the light of day."

I told him, "I don't have the money."

"Shut up, my friend," he replied in annoyance. "You shouldn't be saying that. Do you think everybody who goes there are registered members? You need to think of a way out in every situation. A networker needs to think and creatively come up with possible ways to make things happen."

He continued, "The viable alternative for not having the money to register is to find a registered member whom you can accompany there and gain entrance as his visitor with a token of N500. With the kind of person you are, if you enter there with the perfect game plan, you would have gotten contacts in less than a year who would give you the business that will get you registered in no time."

A good network gives you the power to enter places where on your own, you cannot enter. If you are sales person or a business person, I am certain that you will agree with me that the first hurdle you have to cross to make a sale or get business is to get an appointment to see the key decision maker. You might have a fantastic product, a great idea or wonderful service, which will add value to individuals and businesses. But unless the prospects see you, your products, ideas and service are useless.

You might have good qualification, great competence, fantastic pedigree and so on. Unless the head of recruitment or the chief executive of the company you want to work for sees you or hears about you, you will remain unemployed.

There are four ways of getting others see to you, listen to your presentation and evaluate your proposition. One option is to first write and send a letter/mail and then either place a call or physically visit the place to secure an appointment or check the status of your proposal. The other option is for you to visit the company without any previous communication and ask to see the decision makers. The third option is to have somebody secure an appointment for you and you now go and show up. The last option is to have someone within or outside of the organization take you by hand to the decision maker and have him or her listen to you.

My question is: which do you think offers you better chances of being seen or listened to? I am sure you are torn in-between the third and the fourth options. That is the reward of networking.

Networking gives you the power to enter places where on your own you cannot enter. Networking makes penetration easy. Remember the story of my friend who was only able to gain access to the oil company just because his neighbor called the decision maker and secured an appointment for him.

How many businesses have you lost because you couldn't

get an appointment to see the decision maker? How many of your ideas are wasting because people who need to listen to you have not listened to you? And they have not listened to you because you haven't met them. Is it possible that with your qualification, experience and competence that you deserve better than the place you are currently working and more than you are currently earning? But you are chained because nobody can give you access to the companies that need you? Is it possible that your ideas can solve the economic problem of this country if only the president can grant you audience?

Is it possible that you have the potential to win the Grammy awards if only someone can introduce you to a good record label? Is it possible that you would have been playing in the best team in Europe if only someone introduced you the national team coaches? That is the benefit of networking.

The more you network, demonstrate value and compound your network, the higher your chances of meeting the people that will open doors for you.

Every door has a key and people hold the keys to all the doors.

Your responsibility and my responsibility is to keep making contacts and creating connections until we find the people who hold the keys to the doors we want to enter and make them like us enough to open the doors for us. Networking can help you break protocol.

Reward 7: Achieve your goals and aspirations faster

The seventh benefit is that business and social networking can help you reach your goals faster.

What Contacts And Connections Can Do For You

I had stated in the preface of this book that talent alone cannot save you in today's economy, that good education and qualifications alone cannot save you, that the quality of your product or service alone cannot save you and that the government alone cannot save you.

> **You must add a good network to your talent, to your education, to your competence, to the great ideas and products that you have. You should add a people resource bank, a good support team and good allies.**

For most people, the right network is the missing link between their talent, education, experience, product or ideas and accelerated career and business success. A good network is the missing link between a fat pay cheque and a Salvation Army food.

There are countless stories of people who have not and may not reach their goals because they lack networks that can propel them to advance faster. Great networks are, in my view, business catalysts that ensure you reach your goals faster. I know many businesses that came into being because a man with a dream made a presentation to a network group that believed in him.

While people spend all their lives visiting banks for loans to actualize their dreams, the never-say-die networker simply sends out letters to key people in his or her network, sells the idea to them and the funds come rolling in.

The eight benefit of networking is that a good network can help you help others. How many of your siblings have you helped secure employment because of whom you know? What have you attracted to your community because of people in your network? When was the last time you made a phone call to rescue a friend from a desperate situation? These and much

**Reward 8:
Be a blessing
to others**

more are some of the great things a good well-oiled network can do for you.

How long your younger ones or relatives stay at home after graduating with good grades is to a large extent a function of the quality of your network. How long it takes you to get another job when you lose your job is a function of your network. If your network is not helping you help yourself and others, you either don't have a network or you have the wrong network.

Reward 9: Platforms for making quality friends

The ninth benefit is that business and social networking gives you the power to make quality friends, can provide you with real job security and gives you the power to become better than yourself. Networking also enhances the number and quality of the referrals and advocates you secure.

So even when you are not there and opportunities in your areas of core competence come up, you have people in your network speaking for you. Meanwhile, these are businesses you have been struggling to get by prospecting, booking appointments, making presentations, following up, etc. But just on account of advocacy, these businesses practically look and come for you.

In getting quality friends into your network, you must ensure that you target quality institutions, gatherings and associations to ensure you harvest quality contacts. You cannot expect to play in the big business league if you spend most of your time networking in places occupied by mediocre people, who are beclouded with poverty mentality. With this in mind, you would also be careful where you network and where you spend your time. If you expect to have quality rewards, network where you will find quality people.

Reward 10: Helps you monitor and assess the direction of your life

The tenth benefit of business and social networking is that you can also evaluate the direction of your life by looking at your network. Do your friends and colleagues often complain about the barriers they face in life? Do they often gossip about other people? Do they blame everyone but themselves for their status in life? If these are the kind of people you spend your time with, then of course you are in the wrong network.

Networking helps you increase your chances of meeting people who take responsibility for their situation; who look for solutions, not problems and who are ambitious and determined. People, who face the same challenges that you face, but have a positive mindset. When you meet such people, they will challenge you to drop the self-limiting beliefs that your negative friends have bombarded your mind with. The more you network, the more you meet people of different idiosyncrasies, beliefs, values and ambition. They help you evaluate yourself and circle of friends. Those who limit themselves to few friends and groups loose this benefit of networking.

If most of your friends have not built their own houses, you would think it's okay not have built yours. If most of your friends are having issues in their relationships, you would think it's the norm to have issues; if most of your friends are not meeting their targets at work, you would think that it's a pervasive situation. But when you begin to expand your network, you will start meeting people of your age or younger who have acquired their own houses; you will meet people who are enjoying their relationships; people in the same industry with you who are meeting and exceeding their targets. Please take critical note of this point. Wood destroys wood. Only iron sharpens a ready iron.

No wonder Sandra Renaux stated, "motivated minds networking together can be a powerful force creating desirable outcomes. So, surround yourself with the best possible influences while you strive to bring out the best of each other in your quest for constant and never ending improvement".

Reward 11: Do you like the man in the mirror? The eleventh benefit of business and social networking is that networking will serve as a mirror on the wall for you. When you look in the mirror, the image you see is in the mirror is a reflection of the people you spend your most time with.

At this point, permit me to give you this advice on how to allocate your network.

> I strongly suggest that 50% of your friends, those you spend the most time with and those in your network should be those who are better and more successful than you. They should be those who have achieved most of the things you want to achieve in life. Then, 30% of your friends and in those in your network should be those at the same level with you. And only 20% of the people you spend your most time with should be those that you are better than.

If you spend most of your time with people that you are better than, when you look in the mirror the tendency is to think that you are doing well. When you spend most of your time with people at the same level with you, you would think everybody is facing the same challenges that you are facing. You would think everybody is like you.

However, when you spend more time with people that are better than you, when you look in the mirror, what you will see is what you can become. And that's because people better than you will directly or indirectly challenge and motivate you.

When you spend time with people better than you, you will begin to see how human they are and yet how successful they have become. You begin to learn the principles of success. You see how and why they excel. So you can say to yourself, "if these people can do it, I can also succeed if I am willing to pay the price." Before long, you will acquire the traits and habits of people who succeed.

Reward 12: The power to be bigger than yourself

I remember some years ago when I got referred to a millionaire financial expert who became fond of me. I kept in touch, ensuring I sent him weekly text messages. Surprisingly, one day, he invited me to lunch alongside his millionaire friends.

I did not take the invitation for granted. I was prepared. I was dressed for the occasion. I had plenty of my business cards with me. I did not have money, but I had plans. When we arrived at the lunch venue (wow! what a place!) and sat down, he did an introduction. To my utmost surprise, he announced, "Guys, meet my millionaire friend, Ferdinand." I was not a millionaire yet. I was just a man with a millionaire's mindset. I shook hands with these people and we exchanged cards. That event made me bigger than myself. Since then, we have remained friends and I have done deals worth millions with them.

Some years ago, working in the bank was the in-thing and bankers felt they had job security. Today, many people who relied on such "prestigious" jobs have lost their positions on the payroll, while those who used the platform of their workplace to network

Reward 13. A good network can provide you real job security

have resumed work in new places. So, one other thing that the right network can do for you is that it can provide you real job security.

Reward 14: Strategy for business acceleration

Business success can be calculated. It can be predicted. I can look at your business strategy and tell you where you are most likely to be several years from now. Though many factors contribute to it, but this one factor of networking as a strategy cannot be overstated.

Sometimes, you see business people going around and doing their business without a grasp of the business terrain. They often think they must stumble upon success. The wise business person, the networker, creates an action plan for meeting people who would help his business succeed. A marketer would look for other successful marketers and find out what strategy they applied to succeed.

The wise networker would create a strategy for meeting people that would help accelerate his business success. He would draw up a list of men and women, write out an action plan for meeting them, follow up with them and getting referrals from them.

The business networker realizes that for business acceleration to happen, a strategy of meeting the right people must be penciled down.

ON MARBLE

"Our success has really been based on partnerships from the very beginning."
— Bill Gates

What Contacts And Connections Can Do For You

Chapter 4

The competencies and traits of superior networkers

"The successful networkers I know,
the ones receiving tons of referrals
and feeling truly happy about
themselves, continually put the
other person's needs
ahead of their own."
– BOB BURG

I remember many years ago, I was about to leave my father's house to embark on the journey of my life. It was a significant time, as it probably is in every man's life. A time when you have to move from dependence on daddy to self- dependence. For many, such period of new freedom can be a thrilling time of youthful exuberance and adventurous relationships. You are free from the restrictive regime of your folks; you now dictate your lifestyle and pay your own bills.

Stepping out of daddy's house was no less different for me. I screamed in front of the mirror one morning, "Ferdinand, you have arrived. Your time has come. The world is waiting for you!" I was thrilled at the thought of freedom from the rules and regulations guiding life in my father's house. My dad is a very principled man who firmly expressed his opinions on issues pertaining to my lifestyle with several sayings to support his position.

My life of independence started humbly in a decent Lagos suburban apartment. I moved nothing from my dad's house so I had to acquire new things for myself. The day I moved my personal belongings was a bit emotional for me. Nevertheless, I did not want my folks to see it on my face so that they would not think I was not ready for the move. I put on a show of confidence as I walked around the house smiling. They all laughed when I declared they could visit me anytime provided they informed me well in advance.

Suddenly, my dad announced he wanted to see me in his room for a father-son talk. What I feared greatly was about to happen: another serious talk. "I hope dad does not tell me what would spoil my mood," I mused.

My dad led me into his room and, for the first time, he asked me to sit on the bed. I was almost trembling, as I feared this was going to lead to another hot session. Mentally, I began to shuffle and re-shuffle all my misdeeds to know which could have warranted this encounter and to know what to say in defense.

Dad used to refer to me as a smart kid, as I always had an answer ready for him for every accusation. And being the great communicator he is, he sensed that I was tense. So he doused the tension by stretching out his hands to me in a handshake as he said, "Congratulations, my son! You have made me proud." I was so relieved to hear that. I instantly put up a big grin and replied him with a bemused "Thank you, Dad."

Then he continued, "Ferdinand, my son, while I look forward to the moment you would bring a woman home as your wife-to-be, I must tell you that I am a happy man today. I'm glad that while still under my roof, you saved up enough money to rent a place in Lagos. The very day you mentioned it, I had a feeling of *déjà vu*. It was history repeating itself. I remember telling my parents the same thing so many years ago. Now, my son is doing the same thing.

"You know, life is short. A few people know this. Some years ago, you gained admission into the university. At that time, your every move was based on the money I gave to you or that you swindled me of." We both laughed. "Today you are an independent man. Many of the actions you have taken have made you to become independent. Many of the actions young men of your age take either help them be independent or continue to be dependent on others. I know you are all grown up now and have a mind of your own. I only want to give you a piece of advice that would keep you consistently living a fulfilled life."

The look on my dad's face was different at this time. "My son," he said, "let your ways be pure always."

He went on, "Ferdinand, there are traits for success, there are ingredients for success, and there are requirements for success. Success must be earned. If you are convinced that my blood runs in your veins, your success must be earned. Living alone is one part of the story; the real part, the real you is what counts. Never ignore the fundamentals of success. Never forget them. Your efforts can take you to heights unimagined but only your character would keep you there."

I kept nodding my head as my father spoke to me. He began to cite several examples of men that met their downfall because they ignored the fundamental principles of character, honesty, hard work, respect, commitment, dedication, transparency, relationship. Then he concluded, "My son, money will always come your way when you respect these traits of success. But always remember this: relationship is greater than money."

I responded to the counsel with a "Thank you" in Igbo and thereafter took my leave.

As I walked away from the house, the words 'traits of success' kept ringing in my mind. It was as if my dad's words were transformed into an invisible spider, that spurn a new web of thoughts with each one cleaned out. Those words kept re-echoing over and over. Unconsciously, I began speaking to myself, "Ferdinand, in life there are certain traits you must develop to succeed. If I develop these traits, I will succeed. If I do not, I fail. You must develop these traits."

When I got to my new house, I decided to dedicate a room for personal study. I even put a mirror in the room to have a good view of myself when I begin my self-talk, which I often do to reiterate my commitment to the traits of success.

Dad said, "Value relationships." Sounds funny, but it is true. He also said, "Relationships are greater than money." He meant that great relationships produce great opportunities that result in making money. Poor relationships meant weak potential to succeed.

That day I vowed to build powerful relationships. From that day, I committed my life to being a great networker. I knew I had to develop the necessary skills to become an excellent networker. I began my research by studying notable networkers in the business terrain and I discovered that dad's words were true – many underperforming people lack the traits of effective networking. They expect to succeed, but they lack the ingredients needed to create that success.

> Do you want the rewards of business and social networking? Do you want to enjoy the benefits of and from networking? Hopefully, your answer is a loud and resounding yes. Let me assure you that you can indeed enjoy these benefits and rewards. However, there are competencies and traits you must learn, acquire, develop and master to become an effective networker; so you can enjoy all the fantastic benefits that great networkers enjoy.

What competencies do people who excel in business and social networking possess? We will be examining twenty competencies. Before we highlight those competencies and traits, let's seek to understand the meaning of competence.

When you hear the word competence what comes to your mind? The ability or capability of doing something and doing it effectively. Isn't it? A competent person is one with the ability or capability of doing something, accomplishing a task, delivering on an assignment or role in an effective and efficient manner. My next question is: what do you need to possess to be able or capable of doing something and doing it very well? There are three key things you must have. They are: knowledge, skills and attitude.

For you to be able to deliver on a particular task, there are things you must know about the task, there are skills you must possess and you must have a certain kind or type of attitude. In other words, a competent person is that man or woman who has the required knowledge, requisite skills and right attitude relative to his/her role, task or profession.

On the other hand, an incompetent person is one who lacks the knowledge, the skills and the right attitude to perform. Permit me to state that competence is the difference between 50 years wedding anniversary and divorce after 2 years. Competence is the difference between wealth and poverty. Competence is the difference between meeting your target in the office and being sacked. Competence is the difference between excellence and mediocrity.

Let me buttress these assertions. For you to enjoy a blissful and long marriage as a woman, there are things you must know about your husband, there are skills that you must possess and there are attitudinal dispositions that guarantee joy in marriage. However, if you carry the attitude of a spinster into your marriage for instance, you are heading for divorce.

For you to be wealthy there are things you must know and understand about money; there are money management skills you must acquire. There are also behaviors and habits that lead to wealth, just as there are attitudes that lead to poverty.

For you to meet your target as a sales person, there are things you must know about your prospects and customers, about the economy, about your products and service, about your competitors, etc. You must also possess excellent communication, interpersonal, negotiation, analytical, rapport building and customer relationship management skills. You must have the attitude of patience, persistence, confidence, friendliness and other elements of positive attitude. It's the same principle whether you are a medical doctor, an engineer, a trader, a politician, a soldier or a student.

Let me also add that the depth of your knowledge, your skills set and the consistency in the positive attitude will also set you apart. Meaning that competence also has different levels of proficiency. There is a difference between having basic knowledge about something and being a subject matter expert.

Every superior networker does not only possess the right competencies, they keep striving to improve their level of proficiency. The interesting thing about networking is that the traits and competencies that you require to excel are all learnable and acquirable. In other words, you can learn the act of networking, you can improve your skills as a networker and you can develop a better attitude as a networker.

So, as we begin to highlight the traits and competencies of people who excel in networking, I challenge you to assess and evaluate yourself using the elements I will be pointing out as your benchmark or assessment criteria. Identify the gaps between what you currently know and what you are supposed to know; the gaps between the skills you possess and the ones you ought to possess; your current attitude and the kind of attitude that great networkers have. The difference between what you know and what you ought to know is called knowledge gap. The difference between your current skill set and the ideal skills set is known as the skills gap. Same with your attitude.

Secondly, determine to make whatever sacrifice and to pay whatever price required to bridge the gap, to learn, acquire and develop these competencies. Without these competencies you cannot excel as a networker. And if you don't excel as a networker, you can't enjoy the benefits. Remember that if you cannot pay the price (PRICE), you do not deserve the prize (PRIZE).

TRAIT 1: OTHERS BEFORE SELF

The first trait is that the successful networkers that I know, the ones receiving tons of referrals and feeling truly happy about themselves are those who (according to Bob Burg) continually put the other person's needs ahead of their own. In other words, great networkers are not parasitic and they are not selfish. They do not network with the selfish objective to exploit people. No! They simply realize that man was created to be a social being. So, they are just being natural. They put other people's needs above their own. They continually seek to add value in their relationships.

Would they eventually benefit from networking? Absolutely yes! And there is no apology about that. But there is a wide difference between benefiting from what you do and doing something because of what must get. One is altruistic and the other is selfish. The one who is only interested in receiving will always ask. Give me, help me, show me, take me to, etc. It's about me, I and myself. They will always be desperate. The altruistic ones however understand that if you do not sow, water, weed and tend, you do not deserve the harvest.

> Chatting up somebody in the aircraft should not be because of what you will benefit. Introducing yourself to your neighbors should not be driven by what you can get from them. It should be a natural action consistent with the nature of man. Seek first to network for networking sake; seek first to network so you can add value to people and society; seek first to network and all things shall be added unto you. Great networkers realize this.

TRAIT 2: CLARITY OF PURPOSE

The second trait you must possess to excel as a networker is clarity of purpose. You must clearly articulate your vision, define your mission in life, set clear goals, establish definite objectives and decide your core values. Your vision is your desired future state in life. In other words, it is a statement of what you hope and plan to be in the future. I will come back to the concepts of hope and plan soon. Visioning is about looking at tomorrow and situating your career, your finance, your family and your spirituality in that future. Your vision is your long-term aspiration. You should have clear career vision statement that captures where you want to be in your career in the long run.

You should also have a clear financial vision statement stating how much you want to be worth in terms of investment, real estate, cash, etc. Your family vision statement should state your dream family aspiration in the future, while your spiritual vision statement will state the kind of relationship you want to have with God in the future.

Without a vision, you are like a ship that has set sail without a direction. You are like a football match without goal posts. After articulating your vision statement, the next step is to ask yourself: can I achieve my financial, career, spiritual and family vision with my current set of network? If the answer is no, I am sure you know what to do.

The second element of clarity of purpose is your mission statement. Your mission is the purpose that you serve. The gap that you fill. The service that you render. The value that you add. You cannot achieve your financial vision without serving a purpose, without bringing something of value to the table. You cannot achieve your career vision without playing a role. Same with all other visions you may have. While vision is long term, mission is in the present continuous.

My personal mission statement for instance is "to help professionals improve their personal effectiveness and leadership capabilities." That is the purpose that I serve. That is the gap that I fill in the society. That is the value I offer and sell to individuals and organizations. So, anybody who wants to improve his or her personal effectiveness or leadership capabilities would look for me. Any organization that seeks to improve the personal effectiveness and leadership capabilities of their staff will look for me. It is in living out your mission that you achieve your vision.

Your goals are your short to mid-term aspirations or targets that will sign post the attainment of your vision. So if you have a vision to be financially free before you retire, you should also set mid to short term targets that will sign post that you are on track. For instance, you can set a target of being worth 100 million naira in the next 3 years, having real estate investments worth 200 million in the next 6 years and having stock holdings worth 500 million in the next ten years. They are called milestones. It is only in attaining the mid-term goals that you can fulfill your vision.

Your goals will also include your plans. Your plans should include such questions as: what do I need to do to achieve my goals? Who do I need to know? Who do I need to see? Who are the people that can fast track the achievement of my vision, help me live out my mission and help me achieve my targets? What sacrifices do I need to make? Which organizations do I need to join? What kind of company do I need to keep? Which trainings and skills do I need to get, and so on? Your goals are the operational definitions of your vision and mission. I am sure that you are already seeing the importance of clarity of purpose in networking.

Your objectives should further break down your goals into very short-term activities with deadlines. While in your goal statement, you would have listed the people you need to meet, the organizations you have to join and the value you need to add to actualize your dreams, your objective statements will now set definite activities with the dates, time and places.

So if you identified joining Rotary club as part of the goals you must achieve, in your objective statement, you should now fix a date you will find out the admission criteria, the date you will obtain and submit the completed form, attend the interview, be inducted, etc. That is the difference between your dreams and your plans. Dreams are aspirations without a plan. Plans are aspirations with a strategy.

The final element of clarity of purpose in networking is value. Values are the core principles and convictions that you have. They are the things that you stand on and not willing to compromise. In networking, if you don't stand for something, you will fall for anything. When you begin to network and start meeting people, you will meet those whose beliefs, convictions and dispositions are different from yours.

Sometimes people will ask you to compromise. If you have no clarity about the things you will do and the things you will not do, you would find yourself always doing things that you regret eventually. If you are not careful, people in your network can destroy the reputation you have built over the years, just because you are desperate. Successful networkers know their boundaries. They know the things they will not compromise. They are flexible on issues, but firm on their principles and core values.

A vision without a mission is daydreaming. A vision without goals and objectives is wishful thinking. A vision without core values is watery. Excellent and superior networkers know where they are headed. They know the value they add. They have a clear plan for achieving their vision and fulfilling their purpose. They also know the things they stand on.

Every great networker is a strategist. Their clarity of purpose is guided by carefully devised strategy. For instance:

⮑VISION – I will be the governor of my state.

⮑MISSION – I want to change the lives of the people in my state.

⮑HOW – I will identify contact and connect with the key people that can make things happen.

⮑VALUES – In pursuing my aspiration to be the governor of my state, I am not going to go to a spiritualist, I am not going to join cults, I am not going to change my religion, I am not going to sell my conscience or my values.

⮑GOALS – The first year, I need to register with a political party. I am going to support the local government councilor in my ward. The second year, I need to influence the choice of who becomes the chairman of my local government. By the third year, if I don't contest in the National Assembly Elections, I must influence the nomination of the candidate for that office. By the fifth year, I will become a commissioner. By the sixth year, I will become a Senator, etc.

TRAIT 3: MADLY IN LOVE WITH NETWORKING

The third attribute of excellent networkers is that they love what they do. They love the act of networking. Please take note of this: if you do not have the buy-in for networking, if you do not have deep conviction about the importance and relevance of networking in your life, business and career, please don't bother to network. In networking, you either love what you do or you do what you love. There are no half measures.

Nobody ever excels in networking who does not deeply love the act of networking. And you don't love networking because it is easy to do. Networking has never and will never be easy. As a matter of fact, if networking was an easy thing to do, it won't be worth the while.

The Competencies And Traits Of Superior Networkers

Anything that is easy to do hardly offers any great benefit. That's why it's easier to be poor than to be rich. It's easier to fail than to succeed. It's easier to graduate with a third-class degree than a first class degree. It's easier to fly economy class than to fly first class.

But you know what? It is better to be rich than to be poor; it is more rewarding to succeed than to fail; there are more advantages in graduating with first class than with third class. It is more comfortable to fly first class than economy class.

So successful networkers are not bothered by the inconveniences, challenges, risks and demands of networking. No! They are rather focused on the rewards of networking. I agree that it easier to mind your business than to initiate a conversation with a total stranger because of the likelihood of being embarrassed. I know it is easier to use the thread mill in your house than to join a gym. I know it easier to go back home after service than to wait behind for a meeting of an association in your church or mosque. I accept that it easier indeed to sleep on Saturday mornings than to attend the estate residents meeting. Oh yes, I acknowledge that it is more comfortable to watch movies at home than to be active in your community or alumni associations.

But you know what? If your current lifestyle of isolation has not profited you much, why do you boast in it and about it? Please flee from those who call themselves introverts. Run away from those who say they like minding their business. Keep a distance from those who pride themselves in being alone.

Remember that woe unto him or her that is alone for when he or she falls, there would be no one to bring him or her up. Remember also that those who mind their business too much eventually have no business to mind. You must love and practice business and social networking to the point where you get uncomfortable sitting beside someone without starting a conversation.

You must derive a kick from making new friends. Without being a nuisance to others, you must love being described by people as that friendly, jovial, helpful, intelligent and active gentleman or lady. You must be passionate about networking and that passion comes from the love for networking. Those who benefit from networking just like meeting people, being nice to people, willing to add value in relationships and open to deriving value in return. That is the trait you find in people who excel in networking. You cannot possess what you do not cherish or treasure.

While growing up I was nicknamed parrot because I talked a lot. I talked about everything I saw. My father depended on me to accurately report all the domestic activities when he returned. Even the domestic animals were not spared in my reports. I loved to talk. I developed my talking so well that he appointed me his official reporter of the 9p.m. news whenever he would be late. I played an active role in politics in the university without spending a lot of money, because of my ability to talk my way into people's hearts. I developed a passion for talking. I loved it. I lived it. Today, over seventy percent of my income comes from speaking.

This same principle applies to networking. The first thing you would notice in every super networker is that they love what they do; they love the art of networking. Good networkers do not say things like "I don't like meeting people;" "I don't like crowd;" "I don't like being noticed;" or, "I'm a shy person." Superior networkers know they are a product of both nature and nurture.

Now, nature is the natural thing, the natural endowments that we received from our maker at creation. Our genes, our cells, the composition of our being, the things that we can hardly change, our blood group, our genotype, those are natural things. But beyond these natural things are also "nurtural" things.

The Competencies And Traits Of Superior Networkers

Nurture is what the environment, our background and circumstances have made us. It's the frame of mind we have on account of our experience and background. So, we are all products of nature and nurture. Great networkers realize this and tell themselves, "Even if I'm a shy person, this shyness is a product of nurture." Even if you cannot change the products of nature, you can change offshoots of nurture. I may not be able to change my blood group or genotype, but I can change my communication skills. I can change my attitude towards people in authority. I can choose not to be intimidated when I see people who have achieved a lot of things in life. I can change from being a timid person to being a self-confident person.

The great networkers you see around have gone beyond saying, "I am a naturally shy person" to saying, "I love networking," because they know the benefits of networking. But you have an option; to remain timid and fail to fulfill your potentials or utilize your talents to key into greatness. Or you can make up your mind to say, "I am not going to be shy today. When I have a choice of approaching somebody or retreating, I would choose to meet the person, regardless of the outcome."

Great networkers love to network, because they are aware of its immense benefits. Even if they do not like the very act of networking, they like the benefits. Therefore, they love to do it, not merely to meet more people, but for the benefits and possibilities it leads to.

How many of us love injections, or even pills? I remember a time I was ill in my younger days and I had to visit the hospital. The doctor prescribed some drugs for me to take. I never liked to take pills, unless I was forced to.

My father called me one day and asked, "Would you rather die and not fulfill your potentials because of the two-minute bitter taste of swallowing this Chloroquine?"

That was a turning point for me. That was the day I stopped being scared of drugs. I was willing to take the bitterness of the pill so as to get well. It is the same with networkers. They might not, as a result of nurture, like the art of meeting people or strangers, but they go on ahead to network because they know that the next man has the potential to turn their lives around. They love networking, not merely for the fun of it, but because of what it can do for them.

TRAIT 4: THE WORLD IS WAITING FOR ME TO MANIFEST

The fourth trait of superior networkers is self-belief. They possess a high sense of self-worth. You cannot excel in networking if you have an inferiority complex. Many people want to achieve a whole lot in life, but they lack the sense of self-worth to drive them. The fact that you love helping people, that you have clarity of purpose and that you love networking does not mean that you will achieve your vision by networking if you do not believe in yourself. Every great networker has a large dose of self-belief.

He does not cringe at the sight of meeting people, irrespective of their status in the society. He respects and honors the accomplishments and achievements of others; but they do not intimidate him. He believes that if he does the right things, pays the right price, makes enough sacrifice and remains determined and focused, he can also be successful in life. Rather than cringe at meeting people, he sees himself of having value to add to others. In other words, he believes that it is also in the interest of others to meet him. He approaches you with confidence, not arrogance. He comes with humility, not timidity.

He interacts respectfully, not slavishly. When he meets those that he is better, older, richer or more experienced than, he approaches them with the mindset that he can still learn from others, irrespective of their present status. He does not despise the days of early beginnings. He enjoys the privilege to mentor, guide and help others.

He understands the principle of building and nurturing long-term relationships. He does not wait to live in a good neighborhood before he goes to good neighborhoods to network. He does not wait to be a billionaire before he goes to where billionaires go. He does not wait to buy a big car before he starts attending alumni meetings. He does not wait to be the highest donor before he joins the fund raising committee.

He is fully convinced that what he is today is nothing compared to what he can become in the future. He believes that the world is waiting for him to manifest. He may not be financially rich, yet he knows that his brain is more expensive and better than the most sophisticated computer on earth. He is fully persuaded that he will not give his two eyes for two hundred million euros; that he will not sacrifice his life for a billion pounds.

On account of this self-evaluation, the successful networker steps out to meet people, add value to them and receives value in return. He might not be very wealthy materially today, but he strongly believes that all he needs to become wealthy is time and opportunity. So he maximizes his time and steps out to seek out those opportunities.

Even though he accepts feedback and continuously works on self-improvement, he does not wait for others to validate him. His sense of self-worth is not dependent on other people. He is willing to take no and yet knock on the next-door looking for the yes. He takes rejection, yet asks for acceptance from the next person. He does not ignore his weaknesses, but he focuses on his strengths. He understands that loving self is not selfishness; it is the first step to loving others.

It takes self-worth to walk up to a complete stranger and start a conversation. It takes self-belief to offer to help. It takes self-belief to ask for help. Do you possess this trait? You can acquire it if you don't. How do you increase your self-belief?

ASSIGNMENT

?

This is your assignment. Take a piece of paper and write down the great things you have accomplished in life (like passing your exams, getting promotion, meeting your target, convincing your spouse to marry you against all odds and hurdles from relatives, being the first to buy a car amongst your friends, etc.). Also write down all the compliments you have received from others in the past. Finally, recount the times you started a conversation with a stranger and it went and ended well.

TRAIT 5: HOT AND IMPASSIONED

Great networkers have a fervent spirit. In other words, they are en-thusiastic and passionate. Enthusiasm comes from self-belief. Over the years, I have made presentations to thousands of men and women from different backgrounds. I have also had the opportunity of being a participant at seminars, business presentations and conferences featuring a variety of speakers of repute. I can tell you that there is nothing more irritating than to sit for 10 minutes listening to a boring presentation from a teacher, a salesperson or anyone else.

I often chuckle when a salesperson is trying to make me buy a product he is not enthusiastic about. I am quick to conclude that the product has no significant value to them and they are desperate to dump it on me. I often tell participants in my networking or business presentation sessions that they must never attempt to pass a message across without doing it with passion and enthusiasm. Learn to be inspirational. Let people remember you as a person who charges up the atmosphere.

Every great networker has a fervent spirit. He is enthusiastic, gregarious, joyous, happy, and realizes that happiness and the state of his spirit and mind is a choice. Things might happen to cast him down, but he jumps over them and says, "What has happened has happened. This too would pass away and greater things would happen."

Joy and enthusiasm flow inside him. The things around him are important but he refuses to allow them affect his state of mind. He is consistently happy and he is joyous! You don't see him frowning all the time. He smiles. He has a fervent spirit. He has an outgoing spirit. He is not loud, but he makes his presence felt by his joyous mood. If he were not in a place you would quickly notice it. He does everything with great vigor. He becomes engrossed in the things he does.

People do not like being around those who constantly complain and seeing only barriers. People like to hang around happy and enthusiastic people; people who are positive about life and who see every challenge as an opportunity to excel.

Aura is like a magnetic force. In conventional magnetic force, unlike poles attract and like poles repel. In the case of aura however, like poles attract. So, if, for instance, I'm a happy-go-lucky individual and you are a whiner, there is no way we can be in harmony.

If our auras don't agree, we cannot work together or connect. Consequently, there can't be any networking! Good aura is a product of the thoughts in your head and the feelings in your heart. If you focus on negative things, you will exude negative aura. If you have negative feelings like envy, jealousy, covetousness, malice, etc. you will repel people. That's why some people are not just likeable.

Nobody wants to be around such people. And guess what. These are the ones who complain that other people are arrogant, that successful people are bluffs and that wealthy people are snubs. My dear friend, the problem is with you and in you; not with the successful or the rich. You are manifesting your thoughts. Have you not heard that as a man thinks in his heart, so he is?

Rather than get envious, jealous or angry when you see or meet wealthy or successful people, rather than accuse every rich person of being corrupt, a dupe or ritualistic, be genuinely happy for them. Say to yourself, if they can make it I can also. If you believe that success and wealth can only be achieved by corruption and fraud and you are neither corrupt, nor a dupe, how are you going to be wealthy or successful? When you are around successful people, think success, feel success and talk success. That's the energizer for enthusiasm. Great networkers exude positive energy.

Be happy with every good thing you see, every big house you see, every successful person you see.

TRAIT 6: TIME MANAGEMENT AND SELF-ORGANISATION

The sixth critical element for excelling as a networker is time management and organization skills. I remember the day my son was born. It remains one of the great moments I would live to cherish. When he started crawling, I smiled. Later, with much anticipation, I eagerly looked forward to the day he would walk. And walk, he did! Though he stumbled, I loved the moments of catching him.

All these moments happened in the course of time. I now realize I would never give birth to him again, he would never crawl again, he would never repeat those moments. I needed to be available to witness it to take advantage of the moment. Now time has passed. Those live moments are gone forever.

Time is a critical resource that should be maximized. The same applies to the daily life of a networker. The networker is presented daily with moments to network. Those moments are priceless. While some would maximize them, some would abuse them. Some would take advantage of an opportunity, step up to the potential client, attend that networking event and return that follow-up call. Others will not. Learn to value your time; it's one of your most valuable resources.

Related to effective time management is self-organization. A networker has a daily list of people to see, people to call, people to write and things to do.

Growing up, I learnt memorable lessons about the basics of self-organization. Dad always chided me when I had to do my assignments on the way to school or when I only started to iron my school uniform on the morning before school. I understand better now. We need to plan ahead. Dad often said, "To be ahead, you have to plan ahead." He always said, "A man's natural inclination is to be laid back, to retard, to relax, to procrastinate, to be unserious, to be lazy; but high performers rise above these." These are habits and forces that are determined to keep you from reaching your goals; it is your duty to rise above them through tenacious self- organisation.

Great networkers are very organized and well put together - their thinking, environment, dressing, and everything around them is well managed. Every great networker is a good manager of time. Every great networker is a planner.

Planning, according Alan Laiken is bringing the future into the present so you can start doing something about the future starting from now. The idea behind planning is to ensure that as much as possible, the future unfolds, as you desire it, as you planned. Every great networker brings the future into the present and organizes himself now.

> Great networkers are well organized in all spheres of their life. They know what they would wear for a particular week, what they would do, who they would call, who they would write, and who they would visit. They scarcely forget people's birthdays because they have all relevant events noted in their organizer. They don't forget meetings. They are diary addicts.

Getting organized is about being disciplined and every great networker is disciplined. Every great networker is self-accountable; he takes responsibility; he has standards and he appraises himself by those standards. He also knows certain details about everybody in his network - their birthdays and other important dates.

He has all these, not necessarily in his head, but essentially in his diaries. He is always with a pen and paper. He is always planning and thinking. Self-organization is a critical element you will find people who succeed in networking.

TRAIT 7: I WILL WORK FOR IT AND I WILL WAIT IN HOPE

The eighth trait you will find in successful networkers is patience and persistence. Every great networker realizes that even in the desert if he if digs long and hard enough, he will find water. So if he is drilling for water in Maiduguri and another person is drilling in Lagos, he knows that the man in Lagos is more likely to find water first. But he won't give up because the man in Lagos has found water before him. No! He will keep digging, knowing that it's only a matter of time before he also finds water; and guess what? He is likely to find cleaner water.

A bank Chief Executive shared with us how visited the head office of one the biggest oil companies in Nigeria 103 times before he won the account of the company. Imagine if had stopped at the 100th attempt!

> Patience is the act of waiting. Persistence is doing something while waiting. Some people are patient, but not persistent. Some are persistent, but not patient. Most people walk away from their breakthroughs with just a few minutes left.

This is a generation of fast foods, instant messaging, real time on time banking and do it now. Unfortunately for the "now-now" generation, networking is about patience and persistence. You can't join an association, a club or your alumni group today and expect to hit a jackpot tomorrow.

You might have heard that when you are a good networker, things probably begin to work well for you. Yes, that's true. But that doesn't mean that if you become a networker today, you're sure to become a billionaire in six months. No! It might take you six years!

However, effective networking facilitates the process of achieving your dreams. Networking is not a magic wand that opens all doors and dramatically turns things around. It is a principle, it is scientific, and it is a process. It is a consistent set of actions that you need to do over time, which consequently translates into success.

Don't expect that once you start networking, bingo, your fortune will be delivered to your house the next day. It takes time to build trust.

It takes time to sell value. It takes time for people to understand you enough to let you into their private space. Great networkers are like great sales people.

They know that they may have to knock on 1,000 doors to close 10 deals. So what do they do? They keep knocking. One closed door only takes them closer to a door that will soon open. The great networker knows that in selling, not every prospect will become a customer; yet he keeps prospecting. In geography, there is a concept called weathering. It is the gradual elimination of the rock surface by raindrops. That's the mindset of a great networker.

You have to be patient in building contacts and managing relationships. You must persistent in adding value to those relationships. You must not give up. If you fail on the day of adversity your strength is small. Remember that Patience is waiting. Persistence is doing something while waiting. So if you need to meet somebody, it might take you 1 year to get an appointment or secure access. Persistence is employing all strategies to meet the person, while patience is waiting with the belief that things will work together for your good as you play your part.

Closely related to patience and persistence is hard work, or smart work. Every great networker is a smart and hard worker. He is a smart worker because he uses his brain, and he is a hard worker because he rolls up his sleeves and does what needs to be done.

The great networker realizes that sleep is important, but he would rather delay sleep and do the things that ought to be done now because there would be enough time to sleep later. Every great networker believes in the dignity of labour and in hard work.

Every networker who is a success story today is a networker that thinks more and performs more than others. And if you think and perform more than others, you are certain to excel above them. Every great networker is result- oriented. He is purpose-driven. He is driven by his dreams and he also works out his dreams.

Great networkers believe in the principle of CANI – Continuous And Never- ending Improvement. They are always asking themselves, "What is the next level?" It is not that they are not grateful for where they are, but they know that beyond the current level, there is always a higher level. So they are continuously seeking for and working towards that next level. They are always asking themselves, "How can I improve on my worth and on the value I can add to others?"

TRAIT 8: PUTS THE EAR, MOUTH AND EYES TO WORK

Every great networker has excellent communication skills. It's not about using high-sounding words, but your ability to listen to people. It means to understand the full import of what is said, to read body language and to communicate or give a feedback based on your understanding of your listener's belief or state of mind. That is what communication is all about in networking. In fact, a great networker talks less than he listens; and whenever he speaks, substance proceeds from his mouth.

He knows how to pass his points across in less than a minute, and he listens very well too. He can read moods accurately, knows how to construct his words and seize the moment. Moreover, he can stand on his feet and drive home his point in any gathering.

Some people erroneously believe that good communication is natural. For some people, it is. However, excellent communication is predominantly a result of consistent practice and a willingness to go the extra mile. It's a product of intensive reading and listening. Every good communicator reads voraciously, listens attentively and is conscious of the words he uses.

In networking a good communicator maintains a great sense of humor. Not that he is a clown, but he sees the humorous side of things. He is able to laugh at himself and about life. He knows the one-liners to use in all situations. The difference between humor and clowning is this: humor is all about making people laugh while retaining your dignity. Clowning, on the other hand, is making people laugh and losing your sense of dignity in the process.

TRAIT 9: CULTURAL HUMILITY

Cultural humility means subsuming your culture to the pervading and dominant culture of your environment. It's about aligning yourself to the ways and etiquettes of your environment without compromising your core values, beliefs and principles.

For instance, in the southwest part of Nigeria it is the culture that a younger person should kneel, prostrate or bow the head while greeting an elderly person. In the south east of Nigeria, it is not so. In some environments also, a man is not permitted to shake a woman. In some other environments, you are not just permitted to shake, you are allowed to hug and embrace a woman.

As a networker, you must be culturally aware. You should also be culturally humble. Don't go shaking a woman in the environments where it a taboo simply because your culture permits it. Don't be the first to stretch out your hands to shake an older person in Yoruba land, just because your culture allows it.

Cultural humility is also about making efforts to learn other people's language, eat their food and dance to their music. Like I mentioned earlier on, this is as long your core values and principles are not compromised.

Great networkers understand the fact that you must win the mind share before attempting to win the market share. And there is no better way of winning the mind share than being culturally humble. If you attend a function, where the rule is that people must eat pounded yam with their fingers, don't ask for cutleries. If you enter a place and everybody is sitting on the mat, don't ask for a chair. If the norm in the association that you join is that members call each other by first names, don't introduce yourself and insist you be called by your titles and surname. If the dress code is casual, don't wear your chieftaincy attire with all the beads and feather. That's called cultural arrogance.

TRAIT 10: COURTEOUS

It is apt to discuss at this point, the important role of courtesy in networking. Such words as "Please...", "May I...", "Excuse me...", "Thank you...", "I'm Sorry...", "I Appreciate this...." go a long way in ingratiating one with people. When a great networker finds himself in a situation where he needs to stand for a lady, a kid or the elderly to sit, he would not hesitate to do that.

When a great networker needs to apologize, he apologizes without arrogance. This action comes naturally to him because he knows it is a nice thing to do. Beyond that, it is also a "nurtural" thing to do. In other words, it can be learned and acquired.

TRAIT 11: OPEN HANDS

Generosity is the twelfth trait of great networkers. Great networkers are givers. They are ready and willing to give of their time, energy, prayers, finances and materials. They realize that giving is an honorable thing to do; and that gifts are arrows in the conscience of people.

However, there is a secret to giving in networking. In the religious circle, it is said that the act of giving or that the heart of the giver is more important than the quality or value of the gift. My dear, it is not quite so in business and social networking. In networking, what you give is very important.

Your gift is supposed to serve as a memento and reminder of you before the recipient. Now, if you give me what I would not use, it would have no memorial value. For instance, if you buy someone a cheap shirt that he won't wear, he would simply give it to out because it would be of no use to him. And the giver and the gift would easily fade from the receiver's memory.

Giving in networking is not just about the act of giving in itself, but, more importantly, about what you give. It is about the quality and value of the gift. The secret is this: always give what people would use, so that whenever they use it they would remember you. Do not buy a ₦20,000 wristwatch for someone who would not use it. If ₦20, 000 is your budget for a gift, it is better to ask yourself, "What is the most valuable thing that ₦20, 000 can buy for this person based on his taste, preference and status"?

> **Great networkers have a giving spirit. They just give. They love to tip. Great networkers know that "There is he that scattereth, and yet increaseth, and there is he that withholdeth more than is meet, but tendeth to poverty."**

TRAIT 12: SEE ME, SO YOU CAN HEAR ME

Good appearance is the thirteenth trait you will find in effective networkers. Appearance is very critical in business and social networking because you are seen before you are heard. If your appearance turns me off, then I am unlikely to want to listen to you.

It has been repeated very often that how you dress is how you are addressed. In other words, if my driver dresses very respectably and takes my very expensive car to run an errand for me, people would assume that he owns the car and therefore will address him respectfully. On the hand, if I, the owner of the car dresses shabbily and drives a very expensive car, most people would assume that I borrowed the car or that I am just the driver or mechanic.

Great networkers pay detailed attention to their appearance including the hair, nails, shoes, belts, bags, perfume, clothes, etc. Good dressing in networking is not so much about how expensive your clothes and accessories are; it is more about the quality, the neatness, the fitting on you and the carriage and poise your present. A good dress sense also has to do with dressing right for the occasion. You don't want to go for a beach party with your expensive designer three-piece suit.

Appearance is an offshoot of personal branding. In networking, you dress for where you are going to, not where you are. You dress for who you want to be, not for who you are now. Remember the story of Joseph in the bible? How he shaved and packaged himself to see the king. Didn't he end up as the prime minister of Egypt?

If you want to be a chief executive of a bank, start dressing like one, even though you are just a low level officer. Not necessarily in terms of the cost of the stuff you wear. You don't have to buy the 2,000 dollars suit; but you can get a decent one for 200 dollars. You can get even a tailor to make you a good suit if you can't afford the already-made designer suit. It is called fake-it–until-you-make-it.

If you don't have a good wristwatch, please wear long sleeves and cover your wrist. Don't put on an obviously cheap one. If you can't afford good cologne, use a body roll on. Don't wear cheap perfumes and irritate people's nose. It's all about packaging.

Great networkers have a special set of attire and shoes for certain networking platforms and functions. They know the right things to wear. They know the importance of looking good every day and in everywhere because you never can tell whom you are going to run into. A superior networker doesn't take it for granted that because he is in his vicinity, he can afford to walk around the estate in bathroom slippers.

Effective networking thrives on consistent brand communication. There is constant consideration of people's perception, part of which is derived from how you dress and how you talk. But the emphasis is, first and foremost, on how you dress, since people see you before they hear you.

To the quintessential networker therefore, consistency is critical. He does not want to receive negative comments about his dress sense, or run the risk of running into an important person and realizes that he is not spotlessly suited for the occasion.

> **Before you step out of your house, take a good look in the mirror and ask yourself: 'how much respect will I give to this man in the mirror on account of his appearance?'**

You don't want to attend a function, take a seat besides someone who looks at your shirt, tie, shoes and belt and decides to change her table because you look like a pickpocket or tout.

TRAIT 13: I AM IN CHARGE OF ME

Self-control is the fourteenth trait of great networkers. Every great networker exercises self-control and comportment. They know the number of glasses of wine they must not exceed, so they do not misbehave. They have disciplined themselves not to engage in brawls, no matter the provocation. They do not allow people to influence them negatively. They are in charge of themselves.

Self-control and comportment are directly related to the values and principles that you hold dear. Great networkers know that in networking, they would meet people of different idiosyncrasies, beliefs and values. Now, are they going to subjugate their own values and mannerisms to other people's mannerisms? Are they going to start drinking alcohol and smoking because others do? Great networkers say no to that and people respect them for it.

Great networkers are emotionally intelligent. Great networkers are careful of what they say or do to others. But they also in control of how what other people say or do to them affect them. So while they will not be rude to others, they don't allow the rudeness of others to affect them.

They do not arrogate to others the power of determining their state of mind and actions; such that when others are unhappy, they also become unhappy or when others are rude they also become rude. On the contrary, they hold their own. They refuse to give anyone the permission to control their state of mind. Superior networkers have anger management skills. Please note that your response or reaction to anger is not necessarily caused by what people say or do to you. No. Your response or reaction is a product of the thoughts in your heart. The frame of mind by which you process what is done or said to you.

Let me explain that. If you visit my office on appointment and I keep you waiting at the reception for two hours beyond our agreed time, that would definitely upset you. But if you process the action of keeping you waiting as being because I am genuinely busy, you would show more understanding. However, if you process it to mean that I am disregarding or snubbing you, you will get angry, drop me a stinker of a note and that could possibly destroy our relationship.

If you greet me in the morning and I don't respond to your greeting, you can either interpret my action to be arrogance or believe that I didn't hear you. It is this interpretation at your thought level that would ultimately determine what you do or say to me. Great networkers are in control of their thoughts. Before they draw conclusions, they seek first to understand.

TRAIT 14: I BLOW MY TRUMPET

Self-marketing is the fifteenth trait of effective networkers. Great Networkers are self-marketers. Every great networker knows how to sell him/herself. This is not about boot licking. It's not about sycophancy. It's not about aggressiveness. No! It's about making people know the values you have. It is about making people know the contributions you can make. It is about making people know the gifts and the talents you have. It is about making people know the endowments you have. It's about being assertive.

Networking is about entering a mutually beneficial relationship with someone whereby you are selling and exchanging values. So the person might be a billionaire who helps your business to grow. That is what the person is selling to you. Maybe what you are selling to that person is humour or maybe you advise him on what to wear to events. You probably help him write his speeches or perhaps he just likes you being around him. So, there is a mutually rewarding relationship.

It is not just measured in terms of naira and kobo, in dollars and cents, or pounds and shillings. No. It is also measured in terms of 'do I add any value at all to you? Do you enjoy the text messages I send to you? Or, do you simply enjoy my company?' What I do for you may not be quantified monetarily.

Every great networker knows how to market himself, and knows how to sell the value of the things that he has. He does not diminish the value of his own contribution in that relationship, because it is not measured in fiscal terms. This is the very reason I said self-belief is critical in networking because the very act of self-marketing – selling yourself – is a demonstration of self-belief.

Excellent networkers are always alert to new ideas. They have their ears, eyes and minds open, especially when they are in the midst of people. They are looking for opportunities to offer value, key into something or to demonstrate competence.

TRAIT 15: THINK OUT OF THE BOX OR BREAK THE BOX

Creativity is the sixteenth quality of great networkers. Effective networkers are creative in the way they do things. Creative in how they introduce themselves to others, creative in sending SMS messages or emails. Creative in the way they dress, creative at work, etc.

Creativity, in simple terms, means doing things differently from the way others do them. Great networkers go the extra mile to do things differently. Always keep the creativity question flowing in your heart – how can I give a touch of difference to this matter before me?

If you do what other people do the way they do it, you are no different from them. What can you do creatively? What can you do that would make a whole lot of difference? What investments are you making to improve your creativity power?

Great networkers are problem solvers. They know how to dimension a problem, to identify the root cause of the problem, the impact of the problem, the options available, the advantages and disadvantages of all the options and the best option to adopt to solve the problem. Great networkers believe that within every problem lie solutions and opportunities.

TRAIT 16: GOOD MEMORY

A great networkers have good memory. They develop their memory with relevant memory-enhancing tools and techniques. As an excellent networker, you should possess good, retentive memory. There are so many tools and books you can use for this purpose. Some people meet other people up to five or six times and are still not able to remember the names of these people the next time they meet. Some people don't remember faces!

The ability to remember and retain information, faces, events names and things are not just natural gifts; they are 'nurtural' skills that can be learned and acquired. Your memory can be improved! Some of the tools to help improve the memory include pictures, acronyms, faces, places, events, markers, and so forth.

TRAIT 17: AWESOME ATTITUDE

Prodigious attitude is the eighteenth and perhaps the greatest asset of great networkers. Attitude is simply the voice in your head and how you talk to yourself that determines your response or reaction.

At this point I need to discuss the difference between reacting and responding. If you call me a monkey and I start jumping up angrily asking you why you called me a monkey and even show readiness to fight you, that is reacting. And by the way, doesn't jumping up without control actually validate the monkey you called me? But if you call me a monkey, and I take a look at myself in the mirror and see a good looking man, I will either think you are joking or assume you have lost your senses. That's responding.

Reaction is acting on impulse, more like being influenced by external stimuli.

Responding however, is pondering or thinking through before you take an action. It is your interpretation of the things that happen to you that determines attitude; and your attitude determines your action.

Let me further illustrate this. Two young men are seated beside each other inside a "molue" bus (a notorious means of transportation in Lagos for the poor Nigerians). The bus is over loaded, smelling and very uncomfortable. One of the young men begins to ask himself: what can I do to break out of this poverty, buy myself a car and live a better life? The options begin to come up: save more money, get a better education, start a business, etc. Some of the options could even be negative like: go into illegal business, go into armed robbery or kidnapping. The decision he would make will again be based on how he processes the pros and cons of each option. The bottom line however is that he has placed the responsibility for improving the quality of his life on himself.

On the other hand, the other young man sitting beside him is rather asking himself: why am I poor, who is responsible for my poverty, what I have done to deserve this hardship, etc.? Guess the kind of subconscious answers he will get from these posers? The government is the cause of your problem. Your parents and relatives are responsible. You are unlucky. You have a spiritual problem. Your mother is a witch. Nobody has ever succeeded in your family, etc.

My question to you is: who amongst these two young men is more likely to break out of poverty based on the thoughts of their hearts and the words of their mouth? That's the impact of attitude. Ask and you shall receive means that the quality of your answers is a function of the quality of your questions. If you ask "Why am I poor"? The answers you will get will be the reasons why you are poor. But if you ask, "How can I become rich"?, the answers you will get are the pathway options to becoming rich.

Attitude is the lens through which you look at the world. The cup is either half full or half empty for you. The embarrassments you face during networking, the nos you get and the disappointments you encounter can either be seen as wasted efforts or perceived as stepping-stones to success. You know what? In either case, you are right. If you see them as wasted efforts, you are right. If you see them as stepping-stones to greater things, you are also right.

Attitude is your predisposition or a tendency to respond positively or negatively towards a certain idea, object, person, or situation. Attitude is the mental filter through which you experience the world.

Positive attitude manifests in several ways: they include – positive thinking, constructive thinking, creative thinking, optimism, motivation to accomplish goals despite obstacles, expectation of success and being inspired. Positive attitude helps you to cope more easily with the daily affairs of life. It brings optimism to your life and makes it easier to avoid worry and negative thinking. With a positive attitude you see the bright side of life, become more optimistic and expect the best to happen. It is certainly a state of mind that is well worth developing.

Negative attitude on the other hand is characterized by a great disdain for everything. Constantly pointing out the negative in everything. Once you have a negative attitude, you will be unlikely to recover and self-fulfilling prophecy takes hold.

The person with the positive attitude concentrates on solutions.

The person with the negative attitude dwells on problems. The person with the positive attitude looks for the good in others. The person with the negative attitude finds fault with others. The person with the positive attitude counts his or her blessings. The person with the negative attitude focuses on what's missing. The person with the positive attitude sees possibilities. The person with the negative attitude sees limitations.

◆ ◆ ◆

How to develop a positive attitude

How can you develop a positive attitude that will help you excel in networking and lead you to happiness and success?

* One, choose to be happy.

* Two, look at the bright side of life. If your seven years old son breaks you brand new curve screen television, you can either choose to focus on the TV and the loss, or be grateful to God that you are not one of those childless couples who would happily sacrifice 1,000 curve screen televisions to have one son. If a motorcycle rider hits your car from the back, you can choose to focus on the damaged car and deal with the poor motorcycle rider, or be grateful to God that you are the one that owns a car and not the one riding the bike.
You can either choose to get upset by your husband who snores at night or be grateful that you have a husband. It is not what happens to you that determines your state of mind, it your attitude. The lens through which you see the world.

* The third way to develop a positive attitude is to choose to stay and be optimistic.

* The fourth way is to find reasons to smile. Smiling and laughing

help improve your attitude. 'Yab' and laugh at yourself, so when people 'yab' you, it will have no negative impact on you. Have faith in yourself and the power of God.

◆ That's the fifth way of developing a positive attitude.

◆ The sixth strategy is to contemplate on the futility of negative thinking. Ask yourself, what have I benefited by being negative and focusing on my losses? What have I benefited by being angry?

◆ The seventh strategy for improving you attitude is to associate yourself with happy people. You can't fly with the eagles, if you scratch with the chickens.

◆ The eighth strategy is to read inspiring stories and inspiring quotes.

◆ Number nine way is to repeat affirmations that inspire and motivate you.

◆ The tenth strategy is to visualize only what you want to see happen. Remember that as far as your eyes can see, it shall be yours. Number eleven is to learn to master your thoughts. Your mind is your garden. The manure of your mind is your thoughts. Don't let any thought plant weeds in your mind. Replace any negative thought with a positive one immediately.

◆ Finally, pray and learn concentration and meditation.

These are the traits you find in networkers that excel.

TRAIT 18: EXCELLENT PERSONAL AND WORK ETHICS

The nineteenth quality of successful networkers is that they have good personal and work ethics. Ethics are individual judgments or moral values, which affect personal or professional actions. Work ethics on the other hand is a group of moral principles and standards of behavior or set of values regarding proper conduct in the workplace.

Good ethics in networking include loyalty, honesty, trustworthiness, dependability, reliability, initiative, self-discipline and self-responsibility. Others are attendance and punctuality, character, teamwork, good appearance, productivity, respect, cooperation, demonstrating good manners, respecting confidentiality, seeking opportunities for continuous improvement, obeying rules and regulations.

Great networkers are not perfect human beings, but they strive as much as possible to apply ethics in their conduct and in their relationships.

1. If you face an ethical dilemma in networking my suggestions are:
2. Firstly, talk to people whose judgment you respect.
3. Secondly, ask yourself: what would the most ethical person you know do?
4. What would you do if you were sure everyone would know?
5. Also ask yourself: would I feel comfortable about my professional peers, family and friends knowing about the situation?
6. How would I feel if I saw this in a newspaper?

TRAIT 19: SUBCONSCIOUSLY COMPETENT

The twentieth and final trait that you would find in great networkers is that they have so mastered the previous nineteen traits to the point that have become subconsciously competent. There are four quadrants or levels of competence. They are: unconscious incompetence, conscious incompetence, conscious competence and subconscious competence.

The first quadrant is known as **unconscious competence**. In Pidgin

English, you can describe an unconsciously incompetent person as being: "the person way no know and no know say him no know". In other words, you don't know and you don't know that you don't know. This is the quadrant of ignorance. It can also be described as the quadrant of innocence. For a child it is innocence, because the child is not expected to know. But for the adult, it is ignorance because the adult is expected to know. And that's why in law, an adult cannot plead ignorance in court as an excuse for the breach of the law.

In this chapter, we have highlighted the traits and competencies of superior networkers. Whether you know these traits or not, once you don't apply them, you cannot excel or benefit as a networker.

The second level or quadrant of competence is **conscious incompetence.** This simply means that you don't know and you know that you don't know. In other words, you are aware that there are things you should know, skills you should possess and the attitude to develop if you want to excel as a networker, but presently you have not acquired them. At this point you are aware that knowledge, skills and attitude gaps exist.

This quadrant can be referred to as the learning quadrant. This is where learning starts. You cannot develop any competence until you get to the point where you realize that gaps exist and admit that you need to bridge the gaps to excel.

Learning cannot start unless there is an admittance of deficiency. You cannot improve your communication skills except you admit that your communications skills are not good enough. You cannot learn how to dress better, until you become aware that there is a better way to dress. You cannot improve your attitude unless you get to the point where you realize and admit that your attitude needs to change for you to succeed.

This quadrant is the foundation for developing your competence.

The Competencies And Traits Of Superior Networkers

The nineteen traits of superior networkers we have discussed so far have brought to the fore the competencies you must possess if you are to excel. At this point I expect you to do a self-assessment of your competence using the nineteen traits as benchmark. Has it hit you that your skills need improvement? Have you realized that you need to improve your knowledge? Are you now aware that you need work on your attitude? If your answers to these questions are yes, then you have become consciously competent. You are now ready to learn and grow.

The third quadrant is **conscious competence.** This is the quadrant of **knowledge.** In this quadrant, you know and you know that you know. Here for instance, you know that enthusiasm is important in networking, and so as much as possible you try to become more enthusiastic when you are around people. You now make a conscious effort to dress well when you are going out. You are careful about what you say or do because you know they impact on your effectiveness as a networker.

This quadrant is a very good level to get to, but it's not the ultimate quadrant. Now, you have to think about dressing well to dress well. You have to think about good mannerisms to behave well. At this quadrant, you have probably attended a course or training on networking. You have perhaps bought books and audio CDs on how to network. You have even gone ahead to read and listen to them. So you have head knowledge. You can even show the certificate you were issued on networking; you can brag about the books you have read. To cap it all, you have started practicing the principles of business and social networking.

However, you might still find yourself forgetting to dress well once in a while; you still notice that you have shared a table with someone and not introduced yourself; that sometimes you lose your temper, etc. Do you know why you feel bad after missing the opportunity to practice all that you know? The answer is that you are just consciously competent. You have the head knowledge, but you have not mastered all the traits. You are not perishing for lack of knowledge. You are perishing for the lack of the use of knowledge. The things you know have not become part of you. They have not become habitual. They have not assumed the level of sub-conscious competence.

The ultimate quadrant of competence is **sub-conscious competence.** This is the **mastery** level of competence and proficiency. It is the quadrant of **wisdom**. I like to define wisdom as the constant application of knowledge, until knowledge becomes part of you and profitable to you. If what you know has not become part of you and not profitable to you, it is not wisdom.

Sub-conscious competence is when you have so practiced what you know, the skills you have and the right attitude that they have become part of you. Someone said that excellence is not an act, but a habit. When they become part of you, they become profitable to you. You do them without thinking. This quadrant of competence is attained or achieved by practice and constant practice.

Let's use driving to illustrate this. At a point in your life you didn't know how to drive and you didn't care that you didn't know how to drive. You were unconsciously incompetent. You were ignorant, or perhaps innocent. Then one day, there was an emergency and you needed to take someone dear to you to the hospital. Your neighbor's child hands you the father's car keys to use since the father was not around. But the key and the car are useless to you since you can't drive. Then you suddenly realize that you need to learn how to drive. I will come back to this.

Most people wait until they are in dire states before they acquire the competence, certification or traits that can help or save them. Why do you have to wait until you are told in your office that only those with second degrees will be promoted before you get a second degree? Why do you want to wait until you lose your job before you realize the need to save part of your income? Why do you have to wait until a visitor is on your doorsteps before you tidy up your house?

> Please take this to heart: it is better to be prepared for an opportunity and not have one, than not to be prepared and opportunity knocks and you are not ready. It is better to leave your house with an umbrella and it does not rain, than to leave without an umbrella and it rains.

In other words, it is better to have the competencies and traits for success and not have an opportunity to showcase them than not to have them and they impede you.

Now, back to our driving illustration. Once you realize that you need to learn how drive, you have become consciously incompetent. You now know that driving is a critical skill to possess. But if after realizing the skill gap, you do nothing to bridge the gap, you are as useless as your former state. Which is why I said before that people don't necessarily perish for the lack of knowledge, but for the lack of the use of knowledge. A lot people have read or heard that too much alcohol and smoking are injurious to the health. Some have even lost close relatives because of alcohol and cigarette abuse, yet they indulge in the vices. Their problem is not the lack of knowledge.

Okay, now you have realized the need to learn how to drive and you have also gone ahead to attend driving lessons, pass the driving test and obtain a drivers' license. At this point you have become consciously competent. When you were learning how to drive, you had to look at the gear lever to change the gear. You had to look at the pedal to press the break. You preferred to turn your head to using the side mirrors and you trusted waving your hands to indicate where you were turning to more than using the trafficator.

But after driving consistently and constantly for months and years, you begin to master the art of driving. It will eventually get to the point when you can maneuver the steering with one hand and multi task while driving. What has happened? You have driven consistently until driving has become your second nature. You have become a master and an expert.

At this point you have become sub-consciously competent and you make less mistakes on the wheel. Great networkers know that excellence in networking is not an act, but a habit. You cannot master the traits or competencies of business and social networking unless you constantly practice the things you have learnt.

> **ON MARBLE**
>
> **"Character is so largely affected by association that we cannot afford to be indifferent as to who or what our friends are." - ANONYMOUS**

Chapter 5

Planning for business and social networking

"Before beginning, plan carefully."
– MARCUS T. CICERO."

Over the years, I have been dismayed listening to clients and friends enthusing about what lofty expectations they had for their businesses in the coming year, only to be disappointed because they had no plan in place to actualize their ambitions. Similarly, many networkers find themselves in this distasteful situation: they yearn for powerful contacts, they dream about meeting the movers and shakers in select industries, but hardly have laid out plans for achieving these.

There is no job security these days. We are living in an age of corporate downsizing and freelance consultants. Self-employed workers are increasing by the day. You need an effective networking plan to get ahead and survive in these uncertain times. A deficiency in this regard has restricted promising individuals from attaining their best and has resulted in the death of many great dreams and aspirations.

It is my desire to help you bridge the gap between networking dreams and attainment, using simple methods that would inspire you to take time to plan your networking life for more promising results.

So far, we have examined the meaning of business and social networking; we have also identified the misconceptions as well as the benefits of networking. The last chapter was on the competencies, traits and attributes of people who excel in networking. Hopefully, you now have a clear understanding of what business and social networking actually mean. You must also have been motivated and inspired by the benefits of networking. And of course, at this point you are developing and improving your competencies at the right levels of proficiency.

Expectedly, you are now ready and eager to turn your knowledge into action by launching out to meet people, create connections, build contacts and manage relationships for business and career success. I am indeed excited that you are ready to go.

However, before you set out to network, you must create a plan. As with everything in life, before you start, you should plan. This is even more important in business and social networking. You should first develop your networking plan. We will therefore be focusing on how to plan for networking. But, what is planning?

Planning has so many definitions, but the summary of all the definitions is that planning is deciding in advance what needs to be done and how it would be done. Planning is also the process of setting future objectives and deciding on the ways and means of achieving them. Planning, for networking therefore, is deciding in advance what your future objectives and goals in networking are and how you are going to achieve them.

To plan for networking, there are questions you should ask and answer. The answers therefrom will now form your networking framework and plan. So, please take a sheet of paper and pen and write down these questions. Thereafter, provide answers to them and use the answers to create your definite and workable networking action plan.

1. What Are My Networking Goals?

The first question to ask yourself in planning for networking is: what are my networking goals? Better still, what are my goals in life? I strongly suggest that you break your goals into five broad areas – legacy, career, financial, family and spiritual goals.

Ask yourself: what legacy or legacies do I want to live behind when my time on earth is spent? What do I want to bequeath to generations when I am gone? What visible and memorable contributions do I want to make to my immediate environment, community and society? Those are some of your legacy goals.

The second goal is your career goal. Again ask yourself: what are my career goals? In the next five, ten, fifteen or twenty years where do I want to be in my career? If you are currently in paid employment, how long do you want to remain there; what level do you want to attain and when do you plan to quit? What business do you want to go into when you retire or resign? Where do you want your business to be in the next five, ten, fifteen years? These are part of your career goals.

The third goal to consider is your financial goal. Ask yourself: what do I want to be worth in terms cash, investments, etc. in the next three, five, seven, fifteen years.

For family goals the questions would include: what kind of family do I want to have? What upbringing and level or quality of education do I want for my kids? If you are single, what type of man/woman do I want to marry? What kind of family do I want to build?

Finally and very importantly what are my spiritual goals? What level of intimacy do I want to develop with God? How spiritual do I want to become, as I get older?

❷ What is the Relationship between My Goals and Networking?

Having set these goals, the next question to ask in planning for business and social networking is, "can networking help me achieve these goals?" Further break it down by asking yourself: can I achieve my legacy goals without networking or with my current set of network? Can I achieve my career or business goals without networking or with my current set of network? How critical is business and social networking in the achievement of my family goals? Can I guarantee the quality of life I hope for my family with my current set of network? Can I achieve my financial goals with my current set of network? Can I achieve my spiritual goals with my current set of network?

If you strongly believe that you can achieve your goals in life without people or without networking, then please don't bother to network. But if you believe, or indeed know that you cannot achieve your goals without a good network, you know what to do.

3 *Where Do I Network Now?*

With this question you are simply assessing your current network and your current networking environments. Just review your friends and contact list, examine the people you spend your most time with and assess the places you go to. Then ask yourself these questions: Have I been inspired and, or motivated to dream and pursue my dreams in the places I go to and by the people I hang out with? Who of importance or influence have I met in the places I go to? What quality contacts that would help me achieve my goals in life have I met in the places I go to? How has my life improved on account of the places I go and the people I mingle with?

For the person looking for a wife or a husband, ask yourself: can I meet the type of partner I want in the places I go to? For the person who wants to develop a deeper level of intimacy with God, ask: do I meet people who push me closer to God or people who create doubt in my mind about God in the places I go to? For the career minded person, where do I network now? Can I achieve my career aspirations in the places I go to? Do great business ideas that will help me achieve my financial aspirations flow freely in the places I go to and with the people I spend time with?

If you have more nays to these questions than yes (that is if where you network now does not align with your goals and aspirations) you should quickly consider the next question.

4. Where Should I Network?

If the answers to the question where do I network now does not excite or inspire you, the next natural question should be: so where should I network? The answer to this question is fairly straightforward isn't? Where do the people who need what I have and who have what I want go to? Where do the people who need the value and competencies I have and who have the value that I need go to?

Where would I find the people that would help me achieve my networking goals? Where would I find the people that will help me leave a good legacy and make quality contributions to my community, society and generation? Where would I find the people that would challenge me to pursue my career goals? Where would I find the people that would push me to become more focused, more determined and more competent? Where would I find the people that would inspire me to achieve my financial goals? Where would I find the people that will motivate me to honor my spiritual commitments? Where would I find the people that will help me achieve my family goals?

5. Who Are the Key People I Need to Meet?

Who are the prime people I would love to meet? Where do they go to? What is the best way to meet them? Who can refer or take me to them?

If you are a salesperson, you may need to ask, "Where do my best customers network?" Birds of a feather, they say, flock together. So, the places that your best clients network are where you likely to find people like them.

6. Where Do the People Who Have Achieved What I Want to Achieve in Life Network?

Please remember my advice that 50 per cent of the people in your network should be those who have achieved what you want in life? This should therefore form part of your networking question for your networking plan. Where would you find the people who need to constitute half of your network? Where do they worship, play, gym, dine, etc.?

7. Do I Need a Networking Mentor?

This is particularly important for those who find it difficult to network; including those who say they are shy or reserved. Ask yourself, who amongst my friends or the people I know have good networking skills? Who amongst them have no qualms or inhibitions about walking up to people to initiate and sustain a conversation? Who amongst the people I know embody most of the competencies of good networkers? Who can I call for help?

8. Do I Have Networking Competencies?

Critical competencies to evaluate here are networking skills and the right networking attitude. What skills would you require for business and social networking? Do you have good verbal communication, listening, questioning, interpersonal and rapport building skills? Do you know how to initiate a conversation with a stranger? Do you know how to introduce yourself to a person of status? Do you know how to join a conversation and how to sustain a conversation? Do you know how to end a conversation in such a way that people look forward to meeting you again? Do you know how to secure an appointment and how to follow up?

For attitude, are you assertive without being aggressive? Are you humble without being timid? Are you optimistic, polite and passionate etc.? For the areas where gaps exist, you should ask yourself: what are my plans for bridging these gaps since I cannot network effectively without them? Do I need to attend trainings, read books, listen to tapes, etc.?

9 *Which Organizations Should I Investigate and Possibly Join?*

Would the organizations I am considering joining help me achieve my networking goals? Are their objectives, values and principles consistent with my objectives, values and principles? Who are the members of the association? What are the criteria for membership, including fees and dues? Can I fit my schedule to the program and activities of the groups?

10 *How Many Hours a Week or Month Should I Dedicate to Networking?*

How can I plan and organize myself to balance networking with my other commitments such as family, work and religious demands?

You know for instance that the unmarried lady would have more networking time and platforms for networking than the married woman with kids; the man would also have more networking time than the woman. Your location can also influence where and how long you can network. Other factors to put into consideration are your finances, health, security and competing demands.

11 *Do I Have Networking Tools?*

Networking tools refer to tangible physical things you can use. The important tools to consider are:

- One, your wardrobe. Ask yourself: do I have the right clothes and accessories for the places I want to network and for the kind people I plan and hope to meet? With my current collections, will I be addressed respectfully or treated with disdain? What is the dress code for the gyms, clubs, associations or groups I plan to join?

- The second tool is your business, call or complimentary card. Your complimentary cards are very important tools for networking. You must never be caught without one. As much as possible, you should hand out your business card every time you introduce yourself to a new contact. We will be discussing the importance and how to use your complimentary card in future editions of this program.

- The third tool to consider is your diary. A good, well-bound dairy aids networking. I need to make it clear that the diary is not for taking down sermons and messages in your church or mosque! The diary is for the documentation of appointments and commitments.

  Whenever you bring out your diary and a good pen to note or document an appointment you are consciously or unconsciously conveying to the other person that you are organized, that you are taking the appointment seriously and that since you have blocked that date, the appointment must be honoured.

- The fourth tool is your pen. Please always have a good pen with you. Don't irritate people by always asking to borrow their writing materials.

- The fifth tool is your phone. In these days of mobile phones, you should only have a good phone and you should obey telephone etiquettes.

- The sixth tool is a contact management tool or what you may refer to as an address list. You should have a platform or tool for collecting, storing and retrieving contact information of people you have met and whose details you have collected. We will discuss this in chapter fifteen.

12 Do I Have My Personal Commercial Ready?

Your personal commercial is your introduction of yourself, your name, what you do, what value you add and how you can help. If you have thirty seconds to introduce yourself in an exciting, lucid and memorable way, can you do that? I will guide you on how to develop and master your personal commercial in another chapter of the book.

13 What is My Current Network Comfort Level?

The thirteenth action to take in planning for networking according to Anne Barber is to assess your current networking comfort level by asking such questions as:

- Do I feel professional and comfortable when I am networking?
- Am I energized and excited when I enter a room full of people?
- Is networking something I want to do; not just something I have to do?
- Can I talk easily about my success?
- When I am with people do I find something of interest to me?
- At networking events, can I think of plenty of meaningful topics

to talk about?

- Can I communicate the problems I solve?
- Am I comfortable telling my contacts what I want or need without being beggarly?
- Have I figured a way to learn people's names?
- Have I figured a way of introducing myself to people and make it fun and memorable?

Chapter 6

Where to harvest contacts and connections

"Do not fish for trout in a goldmine
or plough for gold in trout stream."
– ANONYMOUS

We shall now turn our attention to the places to explore for business and social networking. Recall that when we were examining planning for networking I had challenged you to ask yourself: where do I network now? Where should I network? And what organizations or associations should I investigate and possibly join?

What does the saying: "do not fish for trout in a gold mine or plough for gold in a trout stream," mean? It simply means that you should not look for the right things in the wrong places. Do not look for the dead amongst the living. Do not look for a single man in the places where only married men go. Do not look for the rich woman in the places where only the poor go!

The best places to go for networking would obviously be the places where the people and things you are looking for go. I have twenty suggestions.

Networking Place 1:
Your Neighbourhood

Some people live in estates and they do not know the other people within their estate. Some don't as much as know the names of the people living in the same compound with them. The only relationship they have is: "madam, come and move your car, I want to go out". For others the relationship they have is a quarrelsome one. Meanwhile, it possible that the younger brother of the neighbour you are ignoring is the Managing Director of the company you have been applying for a job in. It is possible that your neighbor has information that will solve your most pressing problems. It is also possible that you can help deal with the critical issues facing your neighbor.

There are meetings in your neighbourhood. Attend those meetings. They are potentially powerful avenues for networking. When you attend, tell people who you are, tell them what you do and you could be amazed at the kind of information, contacts and opportunities that will be opened up for you.

Networking Place 2:
Alumni Associations

Are you a member of your secondary school and university alumni associations? Do you play prominent roles? You see, the alumni association has so many advantages. The first advantage is the ease of entry. If you want to join some associations or clubs, the conditions for membership can be very stringent. It is not so with your alumni body. The only criteria or condition for admittance is that you finished or graduated from that school.

Another advantage is that for me, your true friends in life are the ones you made when you were young. The phase in our life when everybody was real. There was no faking, no acting and no pretenses. You bathed naked together in the open bathrooms in schools, you played innocent pranks together and you practically revealed everything about you to everyone. These are friends who knew you at your period of innocence. They also know your strengths.

People you went to school with, or, who knew you when you were growing up, are more likely to give you useful information or do business with you because they have known you right from childhood or school days. It is indeed pathetic that most people do not really exploit the advantages of alumni associations.

My office was once in the same complex with the alumni secretariat of one of the most prominent secondary schools in Nigeria. I was greatly amazed one day to see the caliber of people who came to that building to plan the centenary anniversary of the institution. It was a mind-blowing experience.

However, it is possible that there are lots of people who passed out from that school but are not active in the alumni association. If you ask them why, they would tell you they want to buy a car first before they start to attend the meetings. Whereas, all they need to do is to be active in the alumni meetings and get quality contacts that could give them the business or the job from which they would make the money to buy a car.

There are so many opportunities you can exploit if you join your secondary school alumni association. Your university alumni association is also important. You are availed of useful information, good links and relevant ideas. Somebody once told of how he had tried severally to introduce a product to one of the multi-nationals in the country but could not secure an appointment to see the key decision maker. Despite sending a proposal and requesting for a meeting, nobody was ready to listen to him.

On several occasions, he attempted to see the key decision makers, but the security men always turned him back at the gate and asked him to first secure an appointment. He even asked for the telephone numbers of the person he wanted to see but they would not oblige him. He was rather advised to call the switchboard. Every time he called the switchboard, he was told the person in charge was either busy or not available. He said he went to that company twenty seven times without seeing the person he wanted to see.

After listening to one of my presentations, he said he went and enrolled in his secondary and university alumni associations. The first day he attended the meeting of the University alumni everybody was told to introduce themselves by name, year of graduation and place of work. Surprise, surprise; two people introduced themselves as working in the company he had been trying to penetrate for years. Guess what? One of them was actually the personal assistant to the key decision maker he had been struggling to meet. I am sure you can guess the rest of the story.

Networking Place 3:
Industry Associations

Virtually every profession has an umbrella body. The accountants, the engineers, the lawyers, the doctors, traders, market women, fashion designers, laundry and dry cleaning services, mechanics, hotel owners, speakers, trainers, consultants, barbers, etc. all have various umbrella bodies.

Just like the alumni associations, the only criteria you require to join an industry association is that you belong to that profession. Even if you have to write examinations or tests to qualify for membership, please write those tests and examinations. It positions you as an expert.

The question is: how many people register, attend and participate in such associations? I always tell people that no matter what profession you find yourself make sure you identify, locate and join the umbrella body or association.

Some people are in jobs outside of their field of study. For instance there are lawyers who are working as fashion designers today. My advice to such persons is to join the association for fashion designers as well the one for lawyers. Make yourself very well known in the association, contest the elections and, even if you lose, make sure you make a name for yourself as an expert, a reliable person and an invaluable resource.

Take out time to search for associations that are relevant to your networking plan, know their membership requirements, and get the registration forms. Register appropriately. Be involved. Ask questions. Ask to know how you can be useful to the association. You would be surprised that by volunteering or lending a helping hand, you would gain access to influential people within the association. You must chart your course. See it, move towards it and achieve it. Exploit the platforms.

Networking Place 4:
Conferences, Seminars, Trainings and Workshops

As I stated before, there are so many people who are regretting today because they did not connect with the people they had attended conferences, seminars, trainings and workshop with. Please don't see those platforms as purely knowledge or skills development platforms. Yes, they are; but they are also veritable platforms for meeting people, making contacts and building strong networks. This is more so because those who attend such events already share something in common with you.

There will be many things to initiate and sustain a conversation with. Let me also add that when you attend such events and people are being asked to play roles like coordinator, class rep, rapporteur, etc. please volunteer and play the role very well. Always seek for opportunities to market your competence and value.

Networking Place 5:
Trade Associations

Trade associations, including chambers of commerce are also good networking platforms. Please seek out the ones relevant to your goals and aspirations in life and join them today.

Networking Place 6:
Your Office Environment

If your office is located in a building where you have shared offices or companies, please don't just mind your business. Remember that if you mind your business too much, before long you would have no business to mind. Interact with the people in the same building and even nearby buildings. Get to know them, make them know you, understand their business, find out if there are ways you can be of help and also find out if opportunities exist in their companies that will benefit you or someone you know.

Networking Place 7:
Community Associations

Most communities have development, social or cultural associations in different cities and towns. These community associations are unfortunately neglected by a number of people, particularly the younger ones. They forget that it is possible that there are people who owe their parents favour and who are looking for opportunity to reciprocate for the good deeds of their parents.

They also forget that they may have kinsmen in positions to fast track their careers or businesses. But beyond these benefits is that your community associations provide you the platform to contribute to the development of your community.

Networking Place 8:
Social Clubs

Social clubs are equally good places to network. And just like professional associations, there are lots of social clubs around - Rotary, Jaycees, AIESEC, LEO, Lions, and the like. Some people believe that these social clubs are elitist. Well, even if they were, why not join them and become an elite too. Or don't you want to become one?

It may take some sacrifice to become a member, as the admission process may be expensive, cumbersome or strenuous, but that will become an investment soon enough. The higher the calibre of people in the club, the better for you.

It would do you some good to drive or take a stroll around your neighbourhood during your leisure time to find out if there are social clubs with chapters around you. It is appalling that some people live in certain areas for several years and do not have a grasp of the social clubs in those areas. I am not implying that all social clubs are worthy to be a part of, but once you visit and investigate their activities, you should be able to take a decision on whether joining them will advance your cause or not.

Networking Place 9:
Sports or Hobby-Based Associations

In most cities, there are hobby-based associations like: chess clubs scrabble clubs, tennis, squash clubs, draught and judo clubs, etc. Rather than use the computer to play scrabble, join a scrabble club and play with others as you network. It is better to join a chess club than to play chess with your brother in the balcony.

Your hobbies can be a veritable avenue for you to network. If you play table tennis, for instance, don't just erect a table at your backyard and play only with your kids or relatives. Rather, look for a gym with tennis facility and play there also.

You might have a swimming pool in your house, which is good. But as a networker, you should look for a swimming centre where you can meet people. So, whatever your hobby is, whatever games or recreational activities you are engaged in, rather than doing it alone in your home, look for places where you can meet people who share similar hobbies. It's amazing how the play environment takes away the air of importance that people exhibit in their offices.

Networking Place 10:
Gyms and Aerobics Clubs

Related to hobby-based associations are networking platforms like gyms and aerobics clubs. While it is good and cool to have a well-equipped gym in your house; as well as buy self-aerobics teaching guides, if you are networker you may want to consider joining gyms and aerobic clubs for your exercises. In addition to the networking advantages, I am sure you will be more motivated and challenged to spend five extra minutes on the thread mill, lift an extra kg and stretch a bit more when you see others doing same. The more, the merrier.

Networking Place 11:
Religious Places.

It is baffling how people go to places where the focus is on brotherliness, oneness, love, sharing and giving and yet they fail to connect with others. Some people just go to their places of worship without really exploring the networking opportunities available in their worship environments. They just attend service, give their offerings, do the rounds, perform the rituals and then disappear without as much as exchanging pleasantries with those sitting and shouting amen with them.

In almost every church, mosque or other religious places, there are groups for men, women, single ladies and men, business groups, singers, ushers, teachers and so on. Yet even the ladies who are fasting and praying for a husband will neither join groups nor attend functions for singles.

You can imagine the opportunities open to you if you can showcase your talent and leadership capabilities to a gathering of 500 to 50,000 people. Can you imagine the prospecting and referral opportunities available to you if members of your church or mosque know you, know the value you can add, know the needs you have and know how they can help you?

Networking Place 12:
Parents Teachers Associations (PTA)

Most, if not all schools have functional PTA bodies. Please join such associations and play active roles. If there are activities in the school, endeavor to attend. When you go to visit or pick up your kids or wards from school, interact with other parents, share experiences, connect with them, build and manage the relationship.

Networking Place 13:
Airport Lounges, Train Stations and Bus Terminals

I see people sit in waiting lounges at the airport, train stations and bus terminals waiting for their flights, trains or buses and everyone is just keeping to himself or herself. No interactions, no communications, not even a simple hello. It should not be so. While waiting for your flight, chat up the person sitting close to you. There are so many ways to initiate conversations in such environments, which I will be sharing with you in another chapter of the book.

Networking Place 14:
Inside the Aircraft, Train or Bus

When you now board the flight, train or bus, you are now presented with the fourteenth networking platform. You are travelling from Lagos to China (18 hours) or to New York (13 hours) or to London (7 Hours) or even Lagos to Abuja (1 hour). What do you do? You take your seat, buckle your seat belt, have the free meal, including free red wine, read newspapers, watch movies and sleep; completely oblivious of the person sitting close to you? Meanwhile, it is possible that the person sitting by your right or your left holds the key to your future.

It shouldn't be so.

The aircraft and related environment is a veritable platform for business and social networking. When you board the aircraft, train or bus, the first thing you should do is to greet or say hello to the people sitting closest to you, say something about the trip, aircraft, airline, service etc. If the other party shows interest in your conversation, introduce yourself confidently, get to know the person, evaluate the environment and the person and determine whether you want to exchange call cards. I will provide more details on how to network in various platforms later. The key thing is that you must see the networking opportunity in these places.

Networking Place 15:
Shopping Malls and Markets

Shopping malls, markets and similar environments are the fifteenth place you can also network. When you are in the mall or in the same shop with people, assess the environment, check out the shoppers and decide if it's okay to initiate a conversation. If you think it is okay, you can start by asking questions about their preferences. You can ask them to advice you on the options you are considering. You can offer to help, etc. I need to emphasize that you must be real and not manipulate. Don't go stalking or pestering people. The point I want to make again is that you should watch out for networking opportunities in these environments.

Networking Place 16:
The sixteenth cluster to consider for business and social networking are public meeting places.

These are places like restaurants, bars, cinemas, shows, filling stations, where you pay your bills, where you fix your cars, etc.

Networking Place 17:
Hair salons and Spas

Ladies sit in beauty salons for hours fixing their hair, nails and so on, yet they don't as much initiate a conversation with other people in the salon. The same thing with men. Meanwhile, it is possible that the people you are ignoring need your products, services or ideas.

My advice is that you should be strategic about the salons and spas you go to. It may be better for you to invest a little more money visiting and using salons where the type and kind of people you want to meet go. As a fashioner who designs for the top end of the market, have you considered strategically using salons where your prospects are more likely to be found?

A former Managing Director of a bank told us how while he was a middle level officer in a bank, he used to drive all the way from Ikeja to Ikoyi every two weeks to use a salon where his likely prospects where. According to him, his major breakthrough in banking came from one of the people he met in the salon whom he helped sort out a domestic issue.

Networking Place 18:
Parties and Social Get-Togethers

Please don't just attend a party, eat the food served, drink the wine offered, collect the souvenirs, and disappear. The good thing about such platforms is that people are usually relaxed, willing to mingle and generally happy. Maximize the mood to meet people and make connections.

Place 19:
Social Media

The social media platforms are veritable windows for business and social networking. I have dedicated a chapter of this book on the topic.

Networking Place 20:
Everywhere

The twentieth and most important place to network is everywhere! At almost every instance, you have someone standing close to you, seated beside you, walking towards you or living close to you. Everywhere you find yourself is a potential platform to network, because there are always people to open up a conversation with.

> **ON MARBLE**
>
> "Doing the best at this moment puts you in the first place for the next moment."
> – Oprah Winfrey

Chapter 7

The green and red zones of business and social networking

"Not everything that counts can
be counted, and not everything
that can be counted counts"
– ALBERT EINSTEIN

Let us now turn our attention to the dos and don'ts of networking. The acceptable actions and the taboos of business and social networking. Let's start with the things you show.

◆ ◆ ◆

Green Zone 1:
Network with the
End in Mind

In chapter four of this book, I had listed clarity of purpose as a critical competence of successful networkers. (The elements of clarity of purpose if you remember are: vision, mission, goals, objectives and values). I had also challenged you to articulate and write down your legacy, financial, career, family and spiritual goals. Please note that the essence of that activity was for you to assess your current network to see if it has enough momentum – which is number and quality of people – to help you achieve your life purpose.

When you begin to network, you should always evaluate your networking decisions, actions and investments using your networking goals as benchmark. For instance, you should ask yourself "Will this association I want to join challenge, motivate, inspire or provide me with the platform to achieve my career goals in life?"

◆ ◆ ◆

Green Zone 2:
Believe in Business and
Social Networking

Secondly, you must believe in it. You must believe that it is not good for a man to be alone. Rather, that man is a social being and that two are better than one. You must have a complete buy-in that:

a. Networking is the right thing to do even if there were no benefits.

b. That networking is consistent with the nature of man and

c. That networking will help you achieve your purpose in life.

You should indeed be convinced that networking would work. Conviction is a higher level of belief. It is conviction that produces passion, enthusiasm and positive attitude. If you don't believe that networking will work, please don't bother to start.

❖ ❖ ❖

> **Green Zone 3:**
> **Believe That You Need Networking Platforms to Add Value to Society**

Thirdly, you should believe that you have a lot of contributions to make and value to add to people, your community and society; and that business and social networking will provide you the platform and opportunity to make contributions and add value.

When you now start to network, please keep your eyes on the ball. In other words, target the right people and groups. You are not in it for everybody. Approach only those that are relevant to your legacy, career, spiritual, financial and family goals.

When you join groups or associations, target only the people who need what you have and who have what you need. You probably have knowledge, skills, ideas, products or value that will serve some people; but you also have needs that others can help you meet.

In networking, you can't help everybody. And not everyone can help you. Moreover, you have limited time, energy and resources to network. So be strategic in the choice of the groups you join and individuals that you seek to connect with.

◆◆◆

Green Zone 5: Be Open to All

Yes, we just stated that your should target the right people and groups; but that does not mean that you should despise or ignore anyone. Be polite, courteous, warm and friendly to any and everybody you come in contact with. Meeting, greeting or being polite to people does not mean they are in your network yet.

After the initial interaction, you can now decide what depth or height you want to take the relationship to. You should however try as much as possible to keep in touch; even if it is just virtually and occasionally. The key thing is that you should have a wide network of friends and contacts in diverse groups and fields.

◆◆◆

Green Zone 6: Get it Right the First Time

It is critical that you try as much as possible to get it right the first time. Put another way; make a very good first impression all the time. If you are not certain that you are ready mentally, emotionally and physically please don't step out to network. A bad first impression is like a permanent marker of the board. It will require a lot of energy and chemical to wipe off. And if you are not careful, you would damage the board in the process.

◆◆◆

Green Zone 7: Be a Subject Matter Expert in Something

Assess yourself and identify one area that, either by training or natural talent you are good at; and then build your capacity in that area. There should be something or issues that people will turn to you for ideas or solutions because of demonstrated competence from you.

Be prepared. Be ready and willing to provide insightful answers to issues or questions that people bring to you about your business, your profession or your field.

You can further enhance your reputation as an expert by writing a book (no matter how small), writing articles, and by the quality of your contributions when there are discussions in your area competence. You can also position yourself as an expert by the works that you exhibit and the testimonials from credible individuals or clients.

❖ ❖ ❖

Green Zone 8:
Bring and Add
Value

My suggestion for articulating your value proposition as a networker is to ask these questions:

(a) What issue[s] are facing individuals or groups in my network?

(b) What is the impact of the issue[s] on the individual or group?

(c) How can I help?

(d) Would my solution really deal with the challenges they face?

(e) How do I communicate my solution and make the individual or group believe me?

The key thing in adding value is that you must look out for challenges individuals or groups are facing and be creative in coming up with solutions.

❖ ❖ ❖

God created man with two ears and one mouth. So, we should talk and listen in the same proportion. More importantly, as Stephen Covey would say, listen with the intent to understand. You should actively listen to understand the words, the meanings, the emotion and expectations from the other party.

Green Zone 9: Listen

❖ ❖ ❖

Green Zone 10: Unambiguous Communication

Your communication should be clear and devoid of slangs, jargons and clichés. Make it easy for people to understand you, and the points you are making.

❖ ❖ ❖

Green Zone 11: Keep Your Promises

When you make a promise, keep it. Before you commit to anything as a networker be absolutely certain that you have the time, the energy, resources or whatever is required to fulfill your promise. Remember the principle to under promise and over deliver. It is better to promise to deliver on something in four days, and then deliver in two days. Your trust profile, reputation and integrity are tied to how you honour your commitments.

❖ ❖ ❖

Green Zone 12: Be Ethical

The moral compass with which you decide on good or bad conducts must be such that will endear you to people. Networking ethics include: confidentiality, punctuality, service, integrity, honesty, reliability, courtesy, fairness, timeliness, etc. Abide by them as much as possible.

❖ ❖ ❖

Green Zone 13:
Take it to the
Next Level

Take meeting people to the next level. After meeting someone, please follow up. A phone call, a text message, an email and the evergreen greeting cards are all ways of following up. Whenever you meet and exchange contact details with someone, always follow up. Let them know it was your pleasure meeting them. Thank them.

If they had indicated interest in an area where you have materials on, please send the materials to them. We will discuss how to follow up in details in chapter fifteen of this book.

❖ ❖ ❖

Green Zone 14:
Carry your
referees along

If someone refers you to another person, always keep the referee in the know of your activities, discussions and dealings with the person he referred you to; but without compromising confidentiality and trust.

❖ ❖ ❖

Identify the things you share in common with the people you meet. They are called common denominators. You are more likely to flow with someone you have the same beliefs, values, interests and goals

Green Zone 15:
Focus on Areas of
Congruence

with. So, rather than focus on the things that you differ on, always highlight and reinforce the areas of alignment. Remember that "two cannot work together unless they agree".

❖ ❖ ❖

**Green Zone 16:
Look for Role
Models**

When you network, do not hesitate to walk up to people that inspire or motivate you and tell them so. Fifty percent of your focus in networking should be on meeting and connecting with people who inspire you and who have achieved what you want to achieve in life. Thirty percent should be on building and nurturing relationships with people at the same level with you; and twenty percent of your focus should be on those that look up to you for inspiration, support or guidance.

❖ ❖ ❖

**Green Zone 17:
Pay
Compliments**

Compliments help establish and build rapport in networking. They also help in ingratiating you with people. However, make sure your compliments are genuine. Don't fake it and don't sound patronizing.

❖ ❖ ❖

**Green Zone 18:
Be Real**

There must be no question about your true personality. If you take alcohol and alcohol is served, don't reject alcohol with the reason that you don't take alcohol because you want to impress someone there. You don't want take the risk of being caught by that person one day and somewhere with bottles of beer on your table and a full glass of beer in your hand.

The Red Zone (Don'ts) of Business and Social Networking

Having looked at the things to do as a networkers, let us now identify the things we should not do. Let's call them the taboos of business and social networking.

Taboo 1: Don't assume, believe or think that networking is a magic wand that you can wave and everything will fall in place for you. Oh yes, there are many benefits of and in networking. However, people always get frustrated because they expect too much from networking; even when they have neither developed the competencies nor played their own part in the equation.

Taboo 2: Don't confuse networking with selling. I often chuckle when I meet someone in a party, in the aircraft, in the gym or neighborhood; and less than five minutes after exchanging pleasantries and names he is already trying to sell something to me. This is very common with bankers, insurance sales people and real estate agents. Please don't do that. The networking platform is a contact generating and appointment-securing platform. It is not a selling platform. I am in the party to enjoy myself, not to buy anything. I am in the gym to exercise, not to open a bank account.

Taboo 3: Don't be or appear desperate. Desperation comes with pestering and aggressiveness. If you make a request or someone makes you a promise don't start harassing or pestering the person with phone call calls, text messages and emails. These days, people assume that labeling the communication a "gentle reminder" takes away the sense of desperation. It does not.

Don't also confuse following up with pestering. Pestering is when you remind me of my promise to you in a way that suggests that you don't believe that I plan to honour my commitment to you. It is desperation if you send me repeated text messages or emails mentioning your request to me, or my promise to you. It's also an attack on my integrity; you a casting doubts on my trustworthiness.

Following up however is when you remind of me of you without reminding me of my promise to you. If you send a text message to me once in a while, wishing me well or sending me information useful to me, that's follow-up. You know what? Once I remember you, I remember my promise to you! That's the secret.

Taboo 4: Don't be selfish. People who think only about themselves and how they would benefit hardly enjoy the benefits of business and social networking. Before you talk, listen; before you ask, give. Always look for ways to add value, to be of service, to help others.

Taboo 5: Don't be too quick to ask. Remember that it takes time to build trust. No matter how influential or connected you hear or know someone in your club, association or neighborhood is, don't be too quick to ask for favours, referrals or assistance. Let it develop naturally. Let it flow from casual conversations after rapport and trust have been established. Let it come after you have sufficiently made deposits in the other person's emotional account.

Taboo 6: Don't be a complainer. Avoid being perceived as a faultfinder, a whiner, a gossip, the Mr. Excuse and a rank breaker. People want to associate with barrier breakers not barrier finders. People love solutions providers, not faultfinders.

Taboo 7: Don't pretend or present yourself to be what you are not.

Remember one of our definitions of networking, which is that networking, is a process of building and nurturing long-term relationships. So, if you are in networking for the long haul, you should know that faking and lies would find you out one day.

Taboo 8: Don't take up roles or responsibilities you neither have the competence nor are prepared for. Don't volunteer for assignments just because you want to be seen as being of service when you don't have the capacity to deliver. Don't contest for positions unless you are certain you will commit your time, energy and resources to perform and perform well.

Taboo 9: Don't brag. Don't talk too much about yourself and your accomplishments in a way that may be interpreted as pride, arrogance or boasting. Be careful with the use of titles and nomenclatures when you want to introduce yourself. Who you are is not measured by the titles or positions you occupy. Let your work, your competence and your results speak for you. You don't have to make noise to make news.

Taboo 10: Don't target everybody. Not everybody is in the group for you; and you are not in the group for everybody. Don't over-stretch yourself by trying to be close with everyone. You can be friendly, polite and nice to everybody you meet; but be strategic and focused on the people you really want in your private network.

Taboo 11: Don't talk too much. Don't monopolize conversations and discussions. Don't present yourself as Mr. Know all. Even when you don't agree with other people's position or perspective on issues, you can disagree without being disagreeable.

Taboo 12: Don't force yourself on people. Not everybody will like you. Not everybody would allow you into his or her private space. Don't pry for information about people's personal life. Don't insist that people disclose confidential matters to you. When you ask people question and you have a feeling that they are hesitating or are reluctant to answer, please change the topic.

Taboo 13: Don't label people. Don't use labels like arrogant, haughty, proud, incompetent, etc. to describe people. Even when you have a reason to, don't discuss it with others in your network. It is your personal judgment. Keep it to yourself.

Taboo 14: Don't interrupt. Don't jump into conclusions. Don't tell someone that you know what he or she wants to say. Allow people to state their positions before you respond. One of the ways of achieving this is by mentally taking note of how long it takes you to make your point and then allow the next person a minimum of the time you used to also make his other point.

Taboo 15: Don't discriminate on the basis of religion, tribe, nationality,

gender or other preferences. As long as nobody is forcing his or her preferences on you, you must concede to others the right to be different from you. For instance, if you are empowered or you have the prerogative, don't appoint or choose people to play roles on the basis of the above sentiments. Competence, availability and willingness should guide your choice.

Taboo 17: Don't argue over things you can't change. There are certain sentiments and preferences that people have that you can't change with logic. These are things of the heart, not of the head. For instance, you can't on the basis of logic convince a die-hard Arsenal football club fan that Man United is a better club to support. You can't easily persuade someone who supports a political party to dump his party and join yours.

Networking is not a preaching platform; it is not a debating activity. Networking is a synergy creation activity. Don't start arguments that will alienate you from the people you want to connect with.

Taboo 18: Don't be everywhere and attempt to do everything at the same time. We all have limited time, energy and resources. Don't over stretch yourself by taking up too much. Don't join too many groups or associations. Don't volunteer for too many activities. You may have the passion and competence to do them; but will you have the time and energy?

Taboo 19: Don't look for your honey where you money is. In other words, don't flirt when networking. Decide what exactly your goal is. Are you in it to date all the men in the group or to sleep with as many women as possible? Don't get carried away by the ephemeral things of the heart that you miss the mark. As much as possible, avoid romantic relationships with people in your network; unless of course that is your goal.

Taboo 20: Don't get frustrated because of temporary set-backs. People may disappoint you, breach your trust, humiliate you or embarrass you when you start networking. You should not let any of these discourage you. Don't give up because of temporary set-backs.

Taboo 21: Don't hang out with the wrong people. Who are the wrong people? They are the people who form disruptive cliques, the faultfinders, the negative talkers, the desperate ones; those who are selfish, whose stock in trade are gossip, back biting and envy. Such people hardly bring anything to the table, but they want much. Avoid them like plagues.

These are some of the general taboos to avoid as a networker. These taboos are by no means comprehensive. There may be others based on your location, culture and networking platform. The principal thing is to identify the taboos and avoid them. Mentally accept that breaching these taboos have consequences.

Having said that, also note that if you are new in networking, you may find yourself occasionally breaching some of the rules. If and when you do, please don't let it discourage you or diminish your sense of self-worth. Just learn from your mistakes, determine not to repeat them and move on. With constant and consistence practice, you will become a master networker.

Chapter 8

Networking etiquette for different situations

"Every one of us is an artist, and as an artist, you really can stroll into any venue that you want, as long as you take your time to learn the etiquette of that venue"
– TERRENCE HOWARD

Some years ago, I was invited to a wedding that I was not particularly excited about. However, I chose to attend in order to honour someone dear to me. I did not expect anything inspiring to happen there, but I went all the same with an open mind. As I feared, the event was not in any way fantastic, but I learnt a new dimension to a common concept that day, and that knowledge has remained with me till date.

The chairman of the event advised the new couple to build a lifestyle of service for their union to succeed. He went on to say that his life turned around the moment he stumbled upon this secret. He said, since then, he does not just serve; rather, he serves with style and adds some flavour to whatever he does. His wife calls him the smiling husband, as he smiles often to keep his family happy and excited whenever he is around. As a result, they look forward to seeing him.

By this time, the whole atmosphere seemed charged up already. He concluded by saying, "People become happy around happy people." Getting along is not magic. It requires conscious efforts and fostering on the part of the individuals concerned. I took that piece of advice home and when I opened the door, I put up a large smile and stepped up my excitement quotient.

Have you noticed you when you wear a wonderful smile on your face, you immediately get the same response from the people you're relating with? Have you ever carried a child in your arms with a warm smile? Most times the child smiles back.

Consider this scenario too: you walk past your staff and say, "Good morning, Felicia. You're really looking good today. Beautiful hairdo!" How do you think she would feel? Her attitude to work, particularly on those days of great compliments, will be remarkable. The same rules apply when you're at the receiving end. If you walk up to a teller when you're feeling uneasy and she greets you with an appealing smile and a cheery "Good morning, Sir. You are welcome!" Guess what? Your uneasiness evaporates immediately and you would respond in a courteous way too.

This may not always be the case, but it works in most cases. Cheerful people attract friends quite easily. People want to be around a friendly and courteous person. How you speak, relate, communicate and comport yourself is critical to your success as a networker. In this chapter, we will be considering networking etiquette and the role that courtesy, respect, cheerfulness and concern play in networking success.

Etiquette is the standard of acceptable behavior. According to the Encarta Dictionary, it is the rules and conventions governing correct or polite behavior in society in general or in a specific social or professional group or situation.

Networking etiquette is, therefore, the general rules that regulate networking activities and help networkers to conduct themselves and interact in a socially acceptable manner that makes people feel honored and respected.

Surprisingly, business people often disregard the impact of etiquette on, or importance of etiquette to, business success. Even worse is the fact that most networkers are not grounded in business etiquette as it pertains to today's networker. Some networkers have little thoughts about dress codes for certain events.

As a general rule, have a clean and sharp disposition. Never compromise your outlook. People store a picture of you in their heads. Always ask yourself, "What picture do they have of me in my organization? Can I be nominated, without prior notice, to represent the CEO of my organization at an event? What does etiquette mean to me?"

Sometimes, when the name of a particular staff is mentioned, unpleasant images are stirred up in the minds of people; he is too garrulous, she is dowdy and always unkempt, he has an uncontrollable temper, etc. I remember a mentor calling a staff to order at an event where he was clearly overly loud and expressive, obviously a result of above-the-mark drinking. This show of shame is an example of poor networking etiquette.

There are etiquettes for social, business and networking functions, which are based on guidelines of kindness and respect. The more familiar you are with the etiquette of networking, the more at ease and comfortable you can be when meeting with people. Most of the events where you see people gather have networking potential. And while there, your networking moves should be in line with the specific purpose or theme of the event, be it social or business. The purpose of the event determines what is appropriate to talk about and do at the gathering.

There are different types of conversation that are appropriate for different events. Let us consider a few of them:

★ Social Events

Networking can take place at social events such as weddings, birthdays, retirement parties, anniversary parties, housewarmings, etc. A mentor advised that the effective way to network at social events is to make your networking style gracious. Your networking should be premised on a natural interest in people.

You must attend social events with a networking attitude. This would reflect in your communication. You must be friendly, polite, willing to listen and communicate intelligently. You must be ready to smile, laugh and create an atmosphere that is pleasant. You must understand your limits and respect other people's position. I often advise you wear your garment of courtesy when attending social events. It is always better to consider it an honour meeting other people there. Take attention off yourself long enough to make them feel important, that means you are actually networking. This is one powerful way to relate and connect with people.

★ Business Events

Business events are primarily held for the purpose of giving people the opportunity to meet, get to know each other and discover common areas of interests. The presupposition is that the more connected people feel, the more effectively they are likely to work and enjoy working together.

Business events can be opportunities to engage in business and social conversations. Your sure-bet for acceptance and integration in the stream of the event is to show impeccable manners and ensure your actions and discussions correspond with the overall purpose of the event. These events present opportunities to get away from office conversations and enjoy some informal time with the people you work with or intend to do business with. In these events, people can drop their office persona and discover each other as individuals. Conversations at these events are likely to be about everyday topics and interests like the local news, weather, children, hobbies and sports.

Unfortunately, some networkers do not realize that business events are also very sensitive to business relationships. People never forget a shameful moment as much as they remember a moment you made magical. Never get carried away when you attend a business event. You may meet a company chief executive dressed informally and having fun. As much as you feel free with him, ensure you are professional in your conduct. You are supposed to leverage on this event for a more serious appointment.

I remember a very ugly incidence involving a man and a lady he used to do business with; they were indeed quite familiar with each other. Once he spotted her at a distance, he walked toward her and threw his hands over her shoulder from behind beaming, "Hi love!"

The lady was taken aback. She cast off his hand, while tongue-lashing him to his stupefaction. Unknown to him, the gentleman standing beside the lady was her fiancé, who was equally embarrassed by his action. It pays to always consider the probable effects of our actions beforehand.

★ *Conferences*

Conferences bring people who have common interests together. The best way to get into the flow and make the most of the conference is to be an enthusiastic participant. Be friendly. Generate conversations to find out from people what they are getting – by learning or acquisition – from the conference, what they desire to accomplish at the conference and which other workshop they recommend.

Having learnt that being an enthusiastic participant is the best way to get the most out of a conference, I make it a custom before leaving for any conference to scribble down what I expect to accomplish from that conference. I then use those notes to generate discussions within the small networking platforms that I create at the conference.

Your conduct at conferences should be above board. You should be essentially cheerful, enthusiastic, polite, attentive and willing to learn. Attending conferences, expos and other live events is not just about the presentations of the speakers. Building relationships and discovering potential partnerships are equally vital. And these can only be achieved with the right attitude. The truth is that the right connection made at one of these events could change your life and or your business for good.

Also, business events and conferences present opportunities to meet some of your online friends and colleagues in person. And they are great platforms for building new or consolidating existing relationships. Business success is all about relationships, and having a polished demeanor and social skills position you as a trustworthy and credible person.

★ Charity Events

These are events for raising money for a cause. Some of the discussions at this kind of event border around the difference the cause in question has made or could make in your life, the lives of others or the society generally. Some people have strong desire to actualize dreams they had or causes they cared about while they were growing up and do initiate charity events for them.

Networkers will do themselves a great disservice if they are not conscious of their communication around such people. Bear in mind that they have waited so long to finally live (or fund, as the case may be,) their passions. So, one comment, no matter how innocent, could be a total turn off.

I remember attending a certain charity event where we sat in circles to enable everyone to interact and network. A certain lady, probably in her mid-thirties, was overwhelmed by the influx of donations towards the project and blurted out, "I am sure the promoters of this event would pocket this money for their own selfish interests." Unknown to her, the brain behind the event was seated right next to her. He tapped her lightly and said, "You shouldn't say a thing like that. It's really rude and I am disappointed."

She was even more embarrassed as the gentleman. in his capacity as the convener, was shortly invited to give the vote of thanks. As networkers, we should learn to avoid controversial and sensitive statements in public, since they may result in great embarrassment.

✳ *At a Lunch Invitation*

The main purpose of a business lunch is to meet in an environment that is more relaxed and conducive away from the office. If you are the guest and you are unsure how extravagant you can get with your order, it is best you ask your host what he recommends. His response most times would guide you.

Get along by participating in the general discussion and take it upon yourself that there is no dull moment from the point of making orders. Also, ensure you pay for the meal if you invite someone for lunch or the purpose of that lunch is for your exclusive benefit.

However, if it is a general dining with peers, friends or coworkers, it is common for each person to pay his or her own bill, regardless of who initiated the dinner; except, of course, it is a special occasion such as a birthday or celebration of a promotion. As a rule of thumb, always be straightforward. If you initiated the dinner and are thus responsible for the bill, claim it immediately it is brought to the table.

✳ *Corporate Meetings*

This event brings people together for the purpose of furthering the interests of participating companies, businesses and individuals. This is a perfect networking platform. By being part of this meeting, you are enhancing your visibility in the minds of the other participants. Also, you stand a chance of gaining vital industry information by listening and actively participating in the discourse.

Always ensure that you are active and you liven up the atmosphere of any meeting by sharing experiences and opinions that would trigger similar response from the others. Display of ego at corporate meetings is a betrayal of deep-seated attitudinal problems. And one of its manifestations is seen in baseless arguments that lead nowhere.

★ *Being a Guest or Playing the Host at Events*

A working grasp of the role of a host would go a long way in helping you to manage your guests when you are hosting an event. As host, you are expected to put other people at ease, make them feel taken care of and have that special feeling of being included. The host also takes full control of the event, overseeing all things and ensuring everything runs smoothly and according to plan.

Amongst other things, the host greets people, introduces them to each other and generates common topics for discussions. He generally sees to the smooth flow of the event. The key to success as a host is simply taking your attention off yourself and focusing on your guests.

Ensure you stand up to greet people, unless you are hindered behind tables. Learn to acknowledge the presence of the people around you. Always treat people with equal respect, regardless of their position or status. Most times, you really do not know who that person is connected to, who may have the key to your pot of gold.

As a guest, you must ensure you take light drinks and refreshments. Ensure your business cards are handy. Avoid being loud and do not set out to draw attention to yourself.

However, when you are the guest, you should seek out the host upon arrival and express your congratulations and appreciation for being invited. Do not be an island; mingle and circulate.

◆ ◆ ◆

General Etiquette Tips

Take note of the following etiquette tips to help you make the most of your networking:

1. BE HUMBLE

Don't feel too big to ask for advice on networking etiquette from people who know. Look for a prolific networker and become acquainted with him, so you could learn from him.

2. INTRODUCE YOURSELF

Introducing yourself will afford people the opportunity to know you better. Keep it short and simple; maximum of two sentences. Be sure to ask them what they do and listen to them attentively.

3. SHAKE HANDS

The way you shake hands reveals a great deal about your personality. So, shake hands firmly and warmly, beaming with smiles.

4. POSITION YOUR NAME TAG STRATEGICALLY

Where applicable, position your name tag strategically. Write your first name in capital letters and let your company name be conspicuous as well. If there is enough space you can include your company's tag line.

5. DO NOT FORGET YOUR BUSINESS CARDS

Going to a conference without your complimentary cards is like going fishing without the fishing pole. Your business card is a marketing tool. It is also an extension of you and your company, or the company you represent. Therefore, ensure your cards are clean, free of mutilation and have no notes on the back. When presenting your card to someone, etiquette demands that you present it with the letters facing them.

6. LEARN AND PRACTICE SMALL TALK
Small talk breaks the ice and puts others at ease. Be the first to say "Hello" and then introduce yourself.

7. PUT UP GOOD MANNERS
People will remember your acts of kindness and thoughtfulness more than what you said. Always be polite and considerate of others.

8. SEEK TO ADD VALUE
Seek to give more than you receive: Be a connector. Introduce someone to a person she needs to know. Successful networkers spend considerable time connecting others and being more resourceful than they do looking for clients.

9. DRESS APPROPRIATELY AND BE WELL GROOMED
Your appearance shows potential clients and business associates how well you represent your company. Remember your appearance is what people see first and that is likely to inform a larger percentage of the impression they form about you and the company you represent. You want instant credibility? Create a polished image.

10.BE MEMORABLE
Don't just be another face and number in the crowd. Think of ways through which you can leave a positive, memorable impression. Perhaps you have a signature scarf, pin or hat.

●●●

Common Courtesies

> RESPONDING TO RSVPS

This is a request for a response. When people choose to honour you with an invitation, courtesy demands that you inform them you received their invitation and you would be attending or not attending. It is better to respond immediately you get the invitation by calling, SMS or email. If not done immediately, you may totally forget to respond. It is the same with attending the event: if you do not block the date in your calendar, you may schedule another event or meeting for the same time. Your actions must be prompt.

> MAKING INTRODUCTIONS

As a professional networker, self and people introduction must be your stock-in-trade. In a situation where someone comes over to talk to you while you are already in discussion with someone else, ensure you introduce the new arrival to the person you are discussing with.

Make introductions a fun thing to do. Learn to do it with ease. As a rule, always introduce the younger to the elder, the junior to the senior, the non-official to the official.

The introduction should be done mentioning the name of the person first. Always make the introduction simple, concise and memorable. For example, "Jedichiah, I would like you to meet Peniel. Peniel is the IT Manager of Right Selection Limited and he is thinking of joining our weekend networking club."

> THANK-YOU NOTES

A thank-you note should be kept simple. It should state exactly what you are appreciating the recipient for – thank you for your patronage, the breakfast, the referral, the valuable information, the special time together, and so on.

Consider this example: 'Thank you for introducing me to Bili Odia. I have scheduled a meeting with him for next Thursday and would let you know how it goes. Please know that I immensely appreciate your support and will always treat people you send my way with the highest level of professionalism.'

> ASKING FOR A BUSINESS CARD

Ask for cards naturally. For instance, when someone refers to a subject where you have good information, you can say, "I would like to send you an article on advanced networking tips for branch managers. May I have one of your cards?"

> OFFERING YOUR BUSINESS CARD

Always have a reason for offering your business card. Some funny networkers walk around at events with their cards conspicuously in hand and just dole them out across the audience. Most times, the ratio of the calls received on account of that sharing is low, that is if they are even remembered at all. Always give people a reason to have your card.

Consider this example of offering your card: "Aisha, it's a pleasure to meet you. I would like to follow up with you regarding your seminar that's coming up. If I might have one of your cards – and here's mine – I'd like to get back to you during the coming week."

> TIME MANAGEMENT

Respect people by respecting their time. When you request to meet with someone, go like this, "Can you spare 10 minutes for me to show you how this new iPad works?" or "Charles, is it a good time, or would you like to fix another time for me to call you back?" or "Alhaji, I know your day has been busy. How can I arrange to have about 30 minutes with you?"

When you walk into a person's office, do not just barge in and start talking taking for granted that you are colleagues. Ask for their time and if it is convenient for you to talk with them at that moment. You may be embarrassed if you enter in the middle of a meeting or at a point when some confidential issue is being discussed. Courtesy demands that you knock and wait for a response before going in.

> ### ➤ TELEPHONE ETIQUETTE

Using the telephone can be tricky at times, as you do not see the expressions of the caller or the person you are calling. When on the phone, it is expedient that you are friendly, professional, personable and let people know early enough why you are calling. If, for instance, you are calling someone you were referred to, the following steps would be useful:

- Start by telling the person who referred you to him or her.

- Explain why you were referred to him or her.

- Ask if it is good time to talk.

- If it isn't, ask when it would be more convenient.

- End the call politely. You can say, "Thank you for the opportunity to talk with you. I look forward to calling you tomorrow morning as you requested. Do have a nice day!"

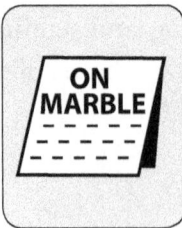

| ON MARBLE | "Position yourself as a center of influence – the one who knows the movers and shakers. People will respond to that, and you'll soon become what you project" – BOB BURG |

PART TWO

How to Network

NETWORK IS NOT ABOUT JUST CONNECTING
PEOPLE. IT'S ABOUT CONNECTING PEOPLE
WITH PEOPLE, PEOPLE WITH IDEAS AND
PEOPLE WIT OPPORTUNITIES.

155

So far in this book we have examined the meaning of networking, the misconceptions about networking, the benefits of networking, the competencies and traits of successful networkers, how to plan for networking and the places to go for networking. We also looked at the dos and don'ts of business and social networking. The last chapter was on networking etiquette.

This second part of the book is the "how to" section. This is the skill part of the competencies that you require to network. In the subsequent chapters of the book I will be examining the real act or practice part of networking. I would like to offer you critical tips that you would find invaluable in your business and social networking sojourn.

We will therefore be focusing on the subtleties of networking success such as: how to initiate a conversation in different situations and platforms including: the aircraft, gym, neighborhood, worship places, mall, bill payment centers, salon, workshops, etc.; how to introduce yourself to people; how to introduce yourself to known personalities; when and how to ask for business cards or contact details; how to sustain a conversation; listening and questioning skills; body language; how to join a conversation; how to respond to the question: "what do you do?"; how to handle lulls in conversation; how to use humor; how to end a conversation; how to ask for an appointment or next meeting; how to follow-up after meeting someone.

We will also be touching on: how to join associations for networking success; what to do when you join; networking ethics and etiquettes; how to communicate and sell value; how to be relevant; how to manage relationships when you join; how and when to make requests, ask for referrals, ask for favor, support, ideas, etc.; how to network in parties, conferences, events, one-off meeting platforms and how to manage contact information. Finally we will be exploring how to use social media for business and social networking.

Chapter 9

How to initiate conversation

"I don't know what he means by that, but i nod and smile at him. you'd be surprised at how far that response can get you in a conversation when you are completely confused."

– JODI PICOULT

One of the biggest challenges faced by those who are fresh in business and social networking is how to approach a complete stranger and open up a conversation. Let us now examine how to initiate a conversation in different platforms and environment.

YOUR NEIGHBOURHOOD

Let's start with your neighborhood. If you have just moved into a new neighbourhood and you want to get acquainted with your neighbours, there are different scenarios that can play out. The first option is to wait until you see them in front of their compound and then you walk up to them with a smile on your face and say something like "I am the newest person in this neighbourhood and my name is.... I live in" You can then give your house number.

The second option is for you to choose a day, preferably Saturday mid-morning or Sunday evening and go and knock at their gates or doors and say something like "hello my name is... I just moved into ...(say your house number and street) and I have come introduce myself to you".

THE AIRCRAFT, TRAIN OR BUS

Next, how do you initiate a conversation with someone in the aircraft? Imagine that you are already seated in the aircraft and somebody takes a seat next to you; or that the person is already seated and you take a seat, our suggestion is that you allow the person to settle down first. Then, you can make a general statement like "this airline has acquired a brand new aircraft" or if the flight was delayed you can say something like "Imagine boarding a 2pm flight by 4pm".

Now, when you are making the statement, you have to make it look like you are talking to yourself; but loud enough for people sitting close to you to hear you. Then wait for any response. If everybody ignores you, you have not lost anything. You weren't talking to anybody in the first place. Just wait for another opening like turbulence or the quality of the meal served to start a conversation with. If however, the person sitting close to you responds to your comment, discuss the issue (of delay, new aircraft) for a while and then say, "by the way, my name is..." and introduce yourself.

I will give you another example. If you seat beside someone in the aircraft or bus and you notice that the person has placed or kept items like phone or wallet in a place where she is likely to forget them, you can also use that to start a conversation. "I hope you won't forget those items?" When the person responds, you can also briefly share your experience of misplacing your item or a story of people who left valuables behind. Listen to her own experience. Then again, midway into the conversation, you can go "by the way, my name is..." and then you introduce yourself.

I am sure you already noticing the sequence. You don't introduce yourself by name before you start the conversation. No! You start the conversation and then introduce yourself by name. I will come to how to say your name soon, but let's look at another environment.

SHOPPING MALL AND SUPERMARKET

Let's assume that you are in a supermarket or a shopping mall and run into someone you have always wanted to meet, or just someone you would like get acquainted with. Let's assume again that the person is picking red apples. You can boldly walk up to the person and politely say something like "hello good afternoon. Please pardon me, but I have always wondered if the colour of an apple determines the nutritional value"?

My experience is that if you are well groomed, confident and polite, most people would give you their perspective. Moreover, people always like to present themselves as experts in nutrition. On the other hand, if you are an expert in that area, you can politely offer your advice on the best item to buy. This can go for buying phones, jewelries, clothes, and shoes; just about anything. Again, take a few seconds or minutes to discuss the product and then go..."by the way, my name is...

PLACE OF WORSHIP, SHOWS, EVENTS AND CONFERENCES
Let's turn our attention to how to initiate a conversation in places like church, mosque, comedy shows, and seminars. For such environments, the easiest way to initiate a conversation is to make a comment about what the preacher, comedian or speaker is saying or has said. For instance, if the priest or speaker says something that appears to resonate with the person sitting beside you, you can turn to the person and say, "that was deep" or "that is so true". If it's convenient, and you are sure you are not distracting or disturbing the other person, you can briefly talk about the point.

In this type of environment however, you don't proceed to introduce yourself by name. Wait until after the programme. If however, both of you are already seated before the event starts, you can turn to the person, say hello and ask the person if he/she has heard the speaker, preacher or comedian speak or perform before. Use that to open a window of conversation and then..."by the way my name is..."

USING COMPLIMENTS
Another way of initiating a conversation is to use compliments. "I like your perfume, your shoes are nice, your hairstyle accentuates your beauty, etc." These are all good one-line compliments that you can use to open a conversation.

> **Remember the golden rule of compliments – the compliment must be genuine.**

Don't just say something nice for the sake of flattering others. If you don't truly believe that the person looks good, you will come across that way.

The second rule is to avoid paying more than one compliment at a time. Don't go... "I like your shoes; your hair is also nice and wow, your bag is awesome". Common, are you inspecting the person? When you pay the compliment and the person smiles and says thank you, the next step is of course to discuss the object of the compliment and then you go..."by the way, my name is..."

Whether you are in the salon, bill payment center, airport lounge or gym, the sequence is the same. Make a general comment, seek or offer advice or pay compliment, then chat briefly and finally introduce yourself by name.

HOW TO INTRODUCE YOURSELF BY NAME

I promised I was going to give you tips on how to say your name when introducing yourself to people. After initiating the conversation and you now want to introduce yourself by name, what do you do? Here is my suggestion.

Look the other person in the face, with a slight smile on your face as you say your name. In saying your name, I strongly suggest that you are deliberate and say your name with dignity. Don't go "I am Ferdinand Ibezim" as if you don't like the sound of your name! How about "I am Ferdinand (a few seconds pause), Ferdinand Ibezim"; or "I am Ibezim... Ferdinand Ibezim."

Repeat the name you prefer to be called twice. And say it like it's the best thing that has happened to humanity after the telephone! Remember James Bond? I am Mr. Bond... James Bond.

Now when the other person says his or her name, please repeat the name the same way the name was said to you without adding or removing any prefix. If for instance the person says, "I am Mike Timothy", say "Oh Mike Timothy, it's nice or a pleasure meeting you". Don't call the person Mr. Michael Timothy when he introduced himself as Mike. If she introduces herself as Patricia Peniel, don't call her Mrs. Pat Peniel. Do you know hundred percent for sure that she is married?

Repeat the name to confirm that the name you heard was the name that was said to you. Don't add prefix or assume the full or shortened form of the name said to you.

HOW ABOUT HANDSHAKES?

It is equally important that we highlight how to give proper handshakes when you introduce yourself to people. Handshake is culture sensitive. Remember that we identified cultural humility as an important attribute of a good networker. Cultural humility is being able to subsume your culture to the culture of the environment where you are networking; as long as the culture does not negatively impact your cores values.

In some cultures, for instance, unless the elderly person first stretches out his or her hand, you do not extend your hand for a handshake. In some cultures, you do not even shake a lady at all. But, in a non-culturally sensitive environment the principle for introducing yourself would be a smile, a straight look in the eyes of the person, an outstretched hand, and then you say your name.

When somebody stretches out his hand to shake you, you should hold the hand firmly. This is not to say that you should do a hand-wrenching grip. But your handshake must be firm and assured. A tentative handshake is a sign of low self-esteem. I am sure you do not want to come across to your new contact as not confident.

Between a man and a lady, the general rule is that the lady should bring out the hand first before the man takes it. It's also not proper to squeeze a lady's hand if you are man. That's not a sign of strength. It's bullying.

Your handshake should convey confidence, not arrogance; humility, not timidity; warmth not flirting. Your handshake is part of the initiation phase of a conversation, exchange of pleasantries and introduction. It should not be extended to the main conversation phase. Calmly withdraw your hand after the introduction and exchange of pleasantries and then continue the conversation.

HOW TO RESPOND TO THE QUESTION: WHAT DO YOU DO?

Nine out of ten times, the people you initiate conversation with and introduce yourself to will certainly ask you "what do you do?" How do you respond when after initiating the conversation and introducing yourself the other person asks you, "what do you do"?

This is an opportunity for you to use your personal commercial. What do you do does not mean, "What is your profession." What do you do does not also mean, "Where do you work?" What do you do means, "What problems do you solve?"

This question is also an opportunity for you to secure an appointment for another meeting. Let me explain that. If I meet two ladies in the elevator or lift, and we start a conversation, and then introduce ourselves by name, and I ask both of them "what do you?" If one of them responds with "I work in XYZ Pensions Company", what is likely to be my reaction? "Oh how about Mr. Tim, your MD or how is your company doing?" This line of conversation is unlikely to lead to another meeting.

However, if the second lady responds with, "I help people retire rich",

I am almost certain to ask her "how do you do that?" If she is a smart networker or a salesperson, that's an opening for her to get an appointment to see me. She can say, "Please I don't want to take your time here, but if I may get your business card I can come in and see you on Monday to demonstrate how we can help you retire rich." What has happened here? She has gotten an appointment to meet me again.

What do you do is about the problems you solve. You do not "do" work in Pension Funds Company. You help people retire comfortably. The place you work is only a platform for solving the problems that you solve or rendering the service that you render.

The essence of a chance meeting and acquaintanceship is to create an opportunity for the next meeting. So, if I ask you what you do and all you say is that, "I'm a banker." I will probably ask you, "With which bank?" And then you will mention the name of your bank. Now, if I already know someone in your bank, I would ask you, "Please, do you know this person?" If you say no, that is the end of the conversation. Even if you respond with a yes, our conversation will at best center on the person that we know. This is unlikely to get you an appointment.

However, if I ask you what do you do, and even though you are a banker, you say, "I help build wealth or I finance projects or I manage assets". Now, you have specifically told me what problems you solve. But, most importantly, I probably would ask you, "How do you do that?" You can now use that window to ask for my business card and get an appointment by saying say, "When can I come to your office and give you more details?" Above all, you would have the time to now go and do a background check on my business and me and prepare a bespoke presentation or proposal.

In my own case, for instance, if you ask me what I do, I will not tell you that I am a consultant. That is probably one of the most abused words on earth. In response I might say, "I create sales champions,

I improve the personal effectiveness and leadership capabilities of people..."

When I say things like that, you are very likely going to ask me, "So, how do you do that?" If we are in a party or conference, I can say to you, "I know you are here to enjoy yourself. Let me not bore you with how we do that now. But, when can I come to your office to make a presentation on how I can create sales champions in your organization?" This kind of flow is called the elevator pitch introduction.

Here is the principle: if you are going with the elevator, it takes about 30 seconds to move from one floor to another. So, if you have 30 seconds to introduce yourself to somebody on the elevator, you have to maximize that time. If the person is going to the first floor and you are stopping at the seventh floor, then you have about 30 seconds to introduce yourself to the person. So, you need to introduce yourself in such a way that the person would give you an appointment for another meeting.

> **The best way to do that is to introduce yourself by highlighting the problems you solve or the service you render. Do not just say, "I'm an accountant. I'm a banker. I'm a fertility doctor." You are not a fertility doctor by way of what you do. Fertility doctor is the title that you are tagged with to do what you do. You do not work in ABC Hospital by way what you do. The hospital only provides you the platform to do what you do. What you actually do is to help people conceive and have children.**

The way you introduce yourself is very important in networking because that meeting on the plane, at the party, at the bar, or at the shopping mall may not be your actual selling platform. It is more often than not an appointment-securing platform

HOW TO INTRODUCE YOURSELF TO A KNOWN PERSONALITY
If you meet a known personality and you want to initiate a conversation with that person the manner in which you will introduce yourself will be a bit different. What you can do is to walk up to the person and pay him a genuine compliment about something he has done in the past; about the success of his business or what he has said before, and so forth. The key here is to ensure that the compliments are genuine. People easily see through insincere compliments that are meant to manipulate them.

Let's assume that you see the Managing Director of a bank that you would like to have in your network, what you can do is to confidently walk up to him with a smile on your face, and say, "Good afternoon, Sir. I'm so delighted to meet you. I am very impressed with what your bank is doing in the banking industry. I like the focus of your bank. I am particularly thrilled with your youth empowerment initiative".

Be specific on the compliment. Say exactly what it is you like about the person or the bank. My other advice is that where possible, and certainly if genuine, pay compliments that will tilt the subsequent conversation around what you do. For instance, if you have an initiative, a product or service targeted at the youths, the last compliment on the youth empowerment initiative of the bank will be very appropriate.

My experience is that nine of ten times you will get a warm "thank you" in return. You can now follow up by saying; "By the way, Sir, my name is...." You can bring out your business card and give it to him. If your card does not explicitly state what you do, the person might ask you, "What do you do?" Even if he does not ask you this, he is likely to ask you what you do for your firm. Do not say, "I am a marketer," or "I'm a risk manager." Use your personal commercial in such a way that you can ask for and secure an appointment for another meeting.

Chapter 10

How to Have and Sustain Good Conversation

"The art of conversation
is the art of hearing as well
as of being heard."
— WILLIAM HAZLITT

am certain that you now know how to initiate a conversation, introduce yourself to people, shake hands appropriately and respond to the question "what do you do?" The next step is how to have and sustain the conversation you have initiated.

Here are some tips:

1. FORGET ABOUT YOURSELF

If you desire to have a good conversation, if you want to sustain the conversation, please forget about yourself. The conversation should not be about you and what you do. Remember that the networking platform is not a selling platform. It's a "get to know you" and secure an appointment for the next meeting platform. So, focus on the other person. The conversation is unlikely to be boring if you focus on the next person.

2. SHOW INTEREST IN THE OTHER PERSON'S INTEREST

Genuinely show that you are interested in what they are saying. A nod, a smile and questions are some of the ways of showing interest.

3. KNOW A LITTLE ABOUT EVERYTHING

One of the best ways to have a good conversation is to, as much as possible know something about everything. That comes from voracious reading, showing interest in lots of things, mingling with people in diverse disciplines and by being inquisitive.

Don't narrow your interest to a few things. Read as much as possible. Listen to as many things as people. Interact with as many people as possible. Be curious. That way, you pick tips, gather information, grab knowledge about many things and you gather things to sustain conversation with people of different backgrounds and disciplines.

Set a target to learn one new thing every week – the economy, politics, law, medicine, philosophy, sports, music and so on. Listen to discussions on radio, watch television and read newspapers. That way you can have something to say about most popular topics of discussion. Nobody is asking you to be a master of all; but you should not be a complete ignoramus in almost everything outside of your core area.

4. GIVE GOOD EYE CONTACT

Look the other person straight in the face without glaring. Relax you demeanor, tilt your head slightly to one side and give them all eye attention. You will come across as timid when you do not look people in the face when you are having a conversation. If you are not comfortable with a straight look in the eyes, you can pick a spot on the face; maybe the forehead or under the eyes to look at. That way, you will still appear focused on the other person.

5. ENCOURAGE THE OTHER PERSON

Show you are listening by nodding and using expressions like: "wow, really, awesome, please say that again, is that so", etc.

6. ASK FOLLOW-UP QUESTIONS

Ask questions arising from what they said. Try and expand their line of thought. Use open-ended questions. And when you ask the question, please shut up and listen to answer. Don't suggest answers in your question. Don't give them options.

Relatedly, if they say things or use jargons or terminologies you don't understand, don't hesitate to seek clarity. Asking for clarifications during a conversation does not diminish you. No! It actually attracts you to people. It shows you are interested in the conversation and that you are humble enough to seek knowledge.

7. ACKNOWLEDGE THE OTHER PERSON

Paraphrase what you just heard. For instance, "Are you actually saying that...?" Also pay genuine compliments for the things your partner says that you find insightful. "Oh, that was deep and very insightful".

"Please I need to write that point down. Please can you say it one more time"?

8. DO NOT INTERRUPT THE OTHER PARTY

Don't tell somebody, "I know what you want to say." That will kill the conservation.

9. BE CAREFUL WITH DISSENTING POSITIONS

If you disagree with the other party's position on a matter, ask yourself "what would I lose if I don't openly show my disagreement or if I let it pass?" For instance what would you lose if he says that Rangers International Club is the best team in Nigeria and you don't argue; even though you are die-hard fan of Kano Pillars?

What would you lose if he says that Lionel Messi is the best player on earth and you don't argue even though you strongly believe that Ronaldo is? You want to establish rapport not to win an argument. If you want to have a good conversation, ask yourself what would I lose if I let his point pass. If the answer is nothing, then don't openly show your disagreement.

> **Remember that a conversation is not a debate or contest that you must win.**

10. TALK LESS

The more you talk, the more mistakes you are likely to make. Remember that when a fool keeps silent he is considered wise, until he opens his mouth.

11. READ BODY LANGUAGE

Pay attention to the things not said. If you are in a conversation with someone and the person keeps looking at a newspaper and talking to you absentmindedly, what he is saying is, "can't you see that my attention is divided? Please give me some peace." You need to be sensitive to nonverbal cues like this.

If you sense the person is getting tired, wants to do something else or perhaps wants to be alone, politely mention your observation and then gradually wind down the conversation. You can have a break and look for someone else to become acquainted with. Even at that, every conversation would come to an end one way or another.

12. DON'T PANIC WHEN THERE IS LULL
A lull is the short or long period of silence during a conversation. You can't possibly chat with someone for two hours without a break. So when there is a lull for whatever reason, don't panic. It's just what it is – a lull.

13. RESPOND TO THE OTHER PERSON
Avoid using one-liners or single words when you are responding. Don't use one liners like: "yes", "no', "not really" to respond to questions from the other party. Don't be too dodgy and at the same time very inquisitive. That's selfishness.

14. KEEP MENTAL AND PHYSICAL RECORDS
Store and note what is being said in your conversation. You may even choose to take notes. You would need this someday.

15. USE INTERESTING STORIES TO SUSTAIN A CONVERSATION
However, make sure your story is exciting, short succinct, clear and unique. Stories always help in sustaining conversations.

16. TALK LESS ABOUT YOURSELF
If you have talk about yourself, do it with humility, use the plural pronoun (rather than say "I made 100 million last year," say "We made 100 million last year" or "Our company made 100 million last year," even if you own the company). If you must talk about yourself,

concentrate on how you can add value to the next person. Whatever you say about yourself should connect with what you are discussing or the questions you are asked.

17. DON'T PRY INTO THE OTHER PERSON'S PRIVATE LIFE WITHOUT ASKING FOR AND RECEIVING EXPRESS PERMISSION TO DO SO

Better still, avoid them at the first meeting. Avoid asking very personal questions or prying into people's private life when you are meeting for the first time. "How's your family" has become a conversational cliché in Nigeria. Now, I am wondering, what if my family brings me sad memories? Do you really want to know?

18. RESPECT PRIVATE SPACE

When you are having a conversation with someone, please respect your partner's space. Don't get too close to the other person. Don't start touching the person. Don't start hitting the other person. Maintain a respectable distance.

19. USE HUMOUR

It is also important that you come in with a sense of humour. A sense of humour is an important attribute of a good networker. But remember that humour is not synonymous with clowning. So, you have to be careful not to offend sensibilities with your jokes. Such topics as sex, gender, religion and politics are sensitive areas to joke about. Be careful about them. Please tread cautiously in these areas.

Nevertheless, humour would always work for a networker. People usually remember the man who made good jokes; who made them laugh in a nice way.

20. WATCH OUT FOR OPENINGS TO SECURE AN APPOINTMENT

If for instance the person says she has been looking for a book on a particular subject, that's an opening to secure an appointment. "I am not promising anything, but if I do get one when and where would be the right time and place to bring the book to you?" If the contact fits into the profile of the network you want to build, then do your best to source and deliver the book to her.

HOW TO JOIN OTHER PEOPLE'S CONVERSATION

Let us now consider a scenario where you have to join other people's ongoing conversation.

Assume you are seated at a banquet or conference table and two people are engaged in a conversation.

It's important to first ask yourself if you really need this conversation; why you should join the conversation, what are they saying and what are you going to say when you join?

For instance, if personal matters are being discussed, such as a lady telling her friend about how her husband hit her recently. That is not the kind of conversation you want to join. You need to establish that the conversation is not personal, nor would it intrude into people's privacy before joning.

Once you ascertain that it's okay to join the conversation, seek the permission of the people whose conversation you want to join before you barge in. You could say something like, "Pardon me, but I couldn't help listening in on your conversation on the economy. This is an issue that interests me greatly. Do you mind if I join the conversation?" If they look at you and turn away, apologize for the intrusion and move elsewhere. However, if they grant you permission to join, make sure your opening statement does not make them wish they had not invited you in.

You should also be careful about taking sides in a conversation you join. If two people have dissenting views about a matter and you want to be part of their conversation, after seeking their consent to join, the next thing you should do is to highlight the critical points of the two parties and then state your own, without appearing to take sides. By so doing, you are showing that you listened to them and that you understand their opinion. Do not join a conversation and put on the air of an expert. You can join as a participant, not as a judge or moderator.

HOW TO END A CONVERSATION

Every conversation will come to an end. But how do you end a conversation memorably? Ending a conversation in networking is different from ending other forms of conversations. Here are some tips for ending a networking conversation.

1. **End Politely.** "It was a pleasure meeting and chatting with you sir". And please say like it you mean it.

2. **Summarize Your Conversation and Show Appreciation.** "I have learnt a lot about malaria from you today. Now I know what to do to prevent it". "I didn't realize that insurance in Nigeria has really improved. I wish other practitioners were as enthusiastic as you. I am particularly attracted to the educational plan scheme". Be specific about your key take away from the conversation.

3. **Explain the Next Steps.** "I will look for the book I promised and send to you". "I will send you the brochure on Monday".

4. **Reconfirm Commitments.** "Please confirm that Thursday is the day I should call you".

5. **Ask for an Appointment**. "I thoroughly enjoyed listening to you madam; please when is the best time to see or call you again?"

6. **Take Your Leave**. If you are in a party or event and you want to meet other people, you can say to the person you have been having a conversation with: "thank you for the privilege of chatting with you, please I need to meet one or two more people before I leave. I promise to keep in touch sir" or "I wish I had more time to enjoy your company sir, but I have to leave now to meet up with some commitments. Have a good day sir".

7. **Look the other party in the face, smile, and where appropriate shake hands and then leave.**

8. **Whatever you do, however you end the conversation, ensure you leave a very good first impression.**

Chapter 11

The role of business cards in business and social networking

"For gosh sakes, it's not a horse race as to how many business cards you can fling out there!"
– BETH RAMSAY

Your business, otherwise known as call or complimentary card is an important tool in networking. Knowing when and how to use it is critical. Your business card typically contains your contact details like: name, company name, telephone numbers, email addresses, physical address, website and for some people, a brief description of what you do.

Your business card is also part of your total package, which is why we always advice that if it is within your control, your business card should reflect your taste, preferences and brand equity. How many times have you received compliments about your business cards?

I believe that as many people as possible should have your business card. Having said that, please note that handing out your business card does not constitute networking. Don't assume that everybody you give your card to has become part of your network or will contact you thereafter.

Your business card is not a flyer or brochure that should be indiscriminately and carelessly shared to everyone and anyone you meet. When you hand out your business card without a definite reason for doing so, eight out of ten times, your card will either end up in a cardholder or in the trash bin; especially if the card is not unique.

The rule is that you don't give out your business card unless you have found some reasons for exchanging phone numbers, names or contact details. So, don't just meet someone and then go straight to your cardholder or pocket to pull out a card even before you start a conversation. The conversation should lead to the exchange of the card. And let the other person know that you have a reason for handing out the card. For instance: "here's my card sir. My contact details are there. Please feel free to call me if you think I can add value to you'.

Meanwhile, the best way to ask for a business card is by giving out yours first. Then you can say after giving out your card, "here is my card madam, please may I have yours". In addition don't ask for someone's business card as if they are doing you a favor. Ask for the card because you want to add value to the person. "I see you are into human resources management. Here is my business card; please let me have yours. I may have some materials to send to you, or if I run into someone who will need your service I will contact you".

When somebody gives you a business card, please don't just put the card in your pocket or cardholder. Take a moment to look at the card; say the name on the card out loud (to confirm that your pronunciation of the name is right) and then say something about the card, name of the person or name of the company. You can go a step further to discuss what the company does. If the card reads consultancy for instance, you can probe further about their area of specialization. It's another way of sustaining a conversation and deepening the rapport.

Meanwhile, if you notice that some contact details are missing from the card, you have to be strategic in asking for them; especially if you are dealing with men or women of status or prominence. If the telephone number for instance is not on the card, you can point at your own card and say, "here's my mobile number on my card madam, I notice yours is not on your card". What you are saying indirectly is, "if you have mine, I should get yours too". My experience is that most people would give you theirs before they think about it. Again, don't ask beggarly!

Once you leave the person, make some notes at the back of the card. Note the venue of the meeting, the event, any interesting thing she said or did, promises you made to her, her commitments to you, date of next appointment, etc. These are information you will transfer to your contact management system after.

Chapter 12

How to Join Associations for Networking Success

"More business decisions occur
over lunch and dinner than any
other time, yet no MBA courses
are given on the subject."
– PETER DRUCKER

I have highlighted the importance of joining associations for the purpose of business and social networking. I had identified associations like: charity inspired associations, alumni associations, industry associations, social clubs, hobby-based associations, community associations and resident associations.

However, before you join it is important that you understand the rules, guidelines and nuances for joining associations for networking success. Let's examine some of them.

Rule 1: Research the Association or the Branch of the Association You Plan to Join

Do a background check of the vision, mission, values, activities and focus of the association you plan to join. Where possible, gather as much information as possible about the pedigree, character and history of the key people behind, and in the association.

Rule 2: Be Strategic in the Choice of the Association and the Branch You Join

This means that you should be certain that the association would help you achieve your legacy, spiritual, career, financial and family goals. Also confirm that the values of the association are in alignment with your core values and principles. Please note that it is possible that the umbrella body of the association might fit into your strategic networking plan, but some branches or chapters of the association may not. Don't assume that every chapter of the association is good for you.

Rule 3: Go to Where Your Prospects Are

Don't get me wrong. We are not talking about prospects in the selling sense. Prospects in networking are people or groups who need what you have and have what you need. You probably want a platform to help the needy or fight a particular course. You will therefore need a platform, group or association whose focus and activities align with this need of yours.

Perhaps you have a message for people of a particular class, age or status. In this case, you will need an association with a large number of the demography your message is for. That is not to rule out the fact that you may also have a product or idea to sell. In this case, you should join an association with a large pool of members that will need the product or idea.

Maybe there are people you want to meet for one reason or the other. In choosing an association or the branch of the association to join, you should also consider all of this. Remember that you cannot pan for gold in a trout stream or look for fish in a gold mine.

Do you have the competencies (knowledge, skills and attitude) to fit

Rule 4: Assess Yourself

into the association you want to join? Do you have the required resources? Can you meet the financial obligations now and in the future? Do you have the right wardrobe? Can you fit your schedule into the association's programmes and activities? Do you have the emotional intelligence to manage members of the association? Do you have, and can you add or sell value to the association and its members when you join?

Rule 5: Have a Game Plan

A game plan is critical. Before you join a group or association, you must have a game plan. What am I implying here? You don't join for everything; you join for some things. So ask, "Who am I here for?" You are not there for everybody. You are there for some people. "What's my value proposition? What's my unique selling proposition? In other words, what will make me positively stand out if I join this association"? "Which sub-group or committee in the association will I belong?" Decide on your investment: time, energy, resources, etc. Then, determine your expected returns before you join.

Rule 6: List Your Networking Options

Use the elements or criteria that we highlighted above to evaluate each option. Establish your Zone of Possible Agreement (ZOPA). Your ZOPA contains the things you would like, the things you can tolerate and the things you CANNOT take. Determine your Best Alternative to a Networking Option (BANO). When you have narrowed down your networking platform options, ask yourself "what's the best alternative to this association I am considering joining. Are there other associations I can also consider joining?"

◆◆◆

RULES FOR JOINING ASSOCIATIONS FOR NETWORKING SUCCESS

Now that you have chosen and joined an association or associations, you should maximize the networking opportunities the platforms present. To do that however, there are some rules and netiquettes you should obey.

1. **Don't expect your paycheck tomorrow.** Don't join as association with the mindset that every member of the association is yours for the taking, or that everybody owes you something. If you come across this way, it won't take long before you are isolated. Your notoriety will spread fast.

2. **Before you benefit, you must commit.** If you want to benefit from an association, you should show commitment to the activities of the association. Attend meetings, events and activities regularly and punctually; pay your dues and contributions promptly,

support other people, volunteer for special assignments and be very visible.

3. **Remember that it takes time to build trust.** Don't expect people to just trust you because you think you are trustworthy. Don't expect people to trust you because you say you are trustworthy, or even because you know that you are trustworthy. Not many people can read your mind or have the gift of clairvoyance. You have to earn the trust; and sometimes it will take time. However, your contacts will trust you if you make them trust you.

Here are some tips for making people trust you:

▸ Do what you say you will do and say what you will do.
▸ Honour your promises, warranties and commitments.
▸ Meet agreed targets and deadlines.
▸ Don't be aggressive and competitive.
▸ Look for collaborations and win-win situations.
▸ Do more than is expected from you.
▸ Don't speak evil of people at their back.
▸ If you have anything about someone, approach the person politely and present your case.
▸ Be reliable every time.
▸ Respect other people's preferences, time, possession relationships and choices.
▸ When you eventually earn the trust, don't abuse it.

4. **Give First.** There are so many things to give in networking – you can give of your time, your advice, material gifts, emotional support, information, referrals, etc. Before you ask for something from someone in the association, try as much as possible to give first. Always seek for opportunities to give. Sow in the physical and emotional bank account of members. You will reap abundantly.

Now, remember that giving in networking is different from giving in religious environments. In networking, you give what the recipient will value and use. So, giving in networking is not a mere activity to fulfill all righteousness. No, giving in networking is a strategic activity done with the aim of embedding you in the receiver's consciousness.

5.   **Be there and consistently perform.** When you join a group or an association for networking, you should endeavor to be physically and mentally present all the time. Don't attend meetings and events sparingly; and don't be absent from meetings without cogent excuses and apologies. When an assignment or responsibility is given to you, first assess yourself to be certain that you have the competence, and that you would have the time and energy to carry it out very well before you accept it. And when you do accept, commit yourself to it.

6.   **Be polite, positive and diplomatic.** Don't come across as haughty, arrogant, self-conceited and lacking in manners. Be slow to speak, quick to apologize, careful in your choice of words, gracious in defeat, easy to express gratitude and show appreciation. When you have to say no, say it with empathy. When you have to disagree with someone, be diplomatic.

7.   **Go for the relationship not the contact.** Making contact is just the foundational stage of business and social networking. The optimum and peak stage is having a mutually rewarding and long lasting relationship. So, your focus should be on developing relationships with the contacts that you have rather than just making contacts. **The work is in the contact; the reward is in the relationship.**

8.   **Be clear about what aspects of your personal life you want people to know about and the ones you don't want to share; and then**

stick to it. Before you divulge very personal information about you, ask yourself, "What would I lose if you don't divulge it now." Some people erroneously believe that one of the ways of achieving intimacy with someone is by rapping about their personal life. Some other people use it to sustain a conversation; while others use the bad things that have happened in their personal lives to seek sympathy. This is a no go area in networking.

The rule is that, unless you are absolutely sure that the other party is now part of your private space, keep personal information, personal. The second rule is that if you don't want more than one person to know, then nobody should know at all.

9. **Let people know that you take notice of them, their appearance, contributions and achievements**. Use compliments, acknowledgements and positive feedback when it is necessary. If someone has made a good speech, walk up to the person and say so. However, to avoid coming across as a busy body, be specific about what aspect of the speech you liked and why. Whenever people go out of their way to do something good, acknowledge them.

10. **Don't talk down on yourself**. Don't say things like, "I am just an ordinary insurance salesperson"; "I don't even have a good work." Don't start a sentence with an apology. Don't imply that what you want to say might not make sense. If you think it would not make sense, then don't say it. Putting yourself down is not humility, it is timidity.

11. **Don't seek for unnecessary attention**. Let your competence, confidence, contributions and ethics speak for you. Don't over sell. Use more "we, us, our, etc." than, "me, I, myself". Don't just stand up to say something, because you want to be heard. Don't over flog your achievements, history and contributions. Be assertive,

not aggressive; be visible, not loud; be audible, don't shout; be popular, not notorious. Remember that you don't have to make noise to make news.

12. **Don't seek to be pitied**. The networking platform is not pity party platform. It's not a baby-sitting center. Don't act is if members owe you anything. People have the right to say no to your requests and demands. Don't take it personal. Don't expect people to go out of their way to help you.

13. **Make yourself approachable**. Plant a permanent and genuine smile of your face. A smile attracts a smile. A frown also attracts a frown. Don't take life too seriously. Don't put up the face of the bad or hard guy. Don't carry yourself as if there are invisible bodyguards surrounding you. An African proverb says that, "it is only when a child stretches out the hand that she is carried".

14. **Model your models**. Imitate the things you see and like in people. We are not advising you to be a copycat; but if you see something good and positive about somebody's actions, comportment, carriage, contributions, etc. model them. Imitate them. Don't be too proud to adapt things that are better than your current state. You can adjust them to fit your unique personality.

15. **Roll up your sleeves and get into the trenches**. This advice is very relevant to the young people. If you attend a meeting or an event of your association and the place has not been arranged or cleaned, role up your sleeves and start doing some work. If you have to call the people responsible to tidy up the place, do so. If you have to do it yourself, do it.

> There's no better description of a networker than, "She is confident, intelligent, well dressed, well-mannered and also humble". Every, and anybody will like you if this is the brand you project. The intelligent, well-mannered, well dressed, confident and humble person.

16. **Don't flirt around.** Don't mistake people's friendliness for looseness. Don't assume that every compliment is an invitation for a night out. Everybody soon knows a flirt's notoriety. Don't look for your honey where your money is. Nothing destroys a destiny more than the lust of the eyes and the lust of the flesh.

17. **Let members know of your competence.** Market your strengths, your knowledge, your skills and your service. Look for opportunities to let members know how good you are in your area of core competence. If you are a painter or sculptor, look for opportunities to exhibit your works; if you are a singer or pianist, seek opportunities to showcase your talent. The best way to do this is to volunteer to do it for free. Make it look like your contribution to the association or service to members. See this action as in investment.

18. **Avoid manipulation.** Don't use deception, misrepresentation and deceit to get things from members.

19. **Avoid borrowing money from members.** You can present business ideas or proposals and ask members of the association to invest. And be upfront about the returns on the investment and the timeline for repayment or dividend. I have come across some people who have lost their reputation and credibility because they went borrowing and soliciting for financial assistance from members telling the same story to everybody.

20. **Don't make unreasonable demands.**

Chapter 13

How to network in parties, conferences, events and one-off meetings

"If your business comes from
relationships, relationships should
be your business."
– DOUG ALES

So far we have examined how to network using associations and membership clubs or societies. In such platforms, you can build your momentum gradually and deliberately. The rules and guidelines for networking in one-off and chance-meeting platforms are slightly different.

If you are invited to a party, a conference or any event and you plan to exploit the opportunity to meet new people, make contacts and expand your network, what do you do? How do you do it? Here are some tips.

1. Pre-Plan the Event

If you are invited to a party or an event, the first rule is pre-plan event. This simply means plan ahead for the event. Do a background check about who is organizing the event, the people invited, the dress code, the sitting arrangements, admission criteria and conditions for entry.

It's important that you find out if there are very important dignitaries who have been invited. Also find out if there are very important government officials whose presence may cause cumbersome security screenings.

For instance in Nigeria and some other climes, if the President or Vice President will be attending an event, some of the roads leading to the venue may be cordoned off, leading to heavy traffic gridlock. In such situations also, nobody is allowed to enter into the venue of the event after the dignitary has taken his or her seat. You don't want to get to the event late or even risk being locked out.

2. Confirm the dress code.

You don't want to look like fish out of water when you get there. Nothing kills the morale and confidence of even the most professional networker more than a poor or wrong appearance.

It's also important to find out who the other invitees are; to confirm if your target audience is listed. If they are, you want to be strategic in positioning yourself where you would meet them.

2. Show Up Early

When you show up early, chat up the event organizers, get friendly with them and ask as many questions as you can about the event, the invitees and so on. Confirm the sitting arrangement. If certain seats and tables are reserved for dignitaries, we advise that you strategically choose a seating position that will give you easy access to the people you want to meet. Also take advantage of your early arrival to engage people as they come in. Do this before the place becomes too busy and rowdy.

4. Dress for the Occasion

Dressing appropriately for the occasion gives you the confidence to approach anybody. Dressing well also makes you more acceptable. Please wear a good, but not offensive cologne or perfume.

5. Be Ready to Move

You are not a matter – having weight and occupying space. Don't wait for people to come to you. Go to them. However, in formal events like conferences and seminars, limit your movement to before the event, during breaks and after the event.

6. Carry More Than Enough Business Cards

We have extensively highlighted how to use your business card. Please refer to that section of this book to refresh your memory. But please always have enough business cards when you are attending parties, conferences or events.

7. Clear Your Head and Mind of Any Worry and Pressure

Remember that you are not there to whine and sulk but to mingle and connect. There is no way you can effectively network if you have a burden on your mind or soul.

8. Be Enthusiastic, Friendly and Approachable
Enthusiasm is a wholehearted commitment to networking. It is the attitude of energetic excitement and interest in your career and life that sets the excellent networker from the mediocre. You must exude a visible deep interest and commitment to what you are doing. You must be amiable, likeable, good natured and easy to relate with.

9. Have Your 30 Seconds Personal Commercial Ready
Your personal commercial includes how you say your name, what problems you solve, what you do and how you ask for appointments.

10. Walk the Crowd at Least Twice
Before you choose a seat at the event, walk the crowd at least twice. Ensure that your choice of seat is not by accident or convenience, but with your networking goal in mind. Don't sacrifice the most important for the least important.

11. Target Your Prospects
Develop, review, adjust, master and trust your criteria for identifying your prospects in a crowd. You are not there for everybody. Concentrate your energy and time on a select few.

12. Don't Spend Too Much Time on One Person
Initiate a conversation, introduce yourself, briefly sustain the conversation to identify common grounds, look for opportunities to be of service, exchange contact details, agree when to reconnect and move on.

13. Split Up
When you attend parties, conferences or similar one off events please split up. Split up means don't seat on the same table with the people you went to the event with. Unless it is a reserved table, I hate to see

people working in the same company sitting on the same table at an event. As much as possible don't sit on the same table or hang around with people that are already in your network.

Avoid spending more than a few seconds with colleagues at work, relatives and friends that you are in regular contact with. The successful networker's radar is always on new contacts, deepening or cementing old, but not yet familiar contacts; not on catching up with old folks and pals.

14. Do Not Butt In

When you attend events or parties and people are having a conversation, don't jump in. Do not interrupt other people's conversations. Don't join conversations without asking and getting the permission of the people involved.

15. Don't Get Drunk

Don't even get tipsy. It is better to remain sober and clear-headed throughout the event than to get tipsy or drunk. The risk is that you can get loose with your actions and words when you are under the influence of alcohol.

16. Don't Be Distracted by the Food Served

We always advise young networkers to eat before attending events. That way, you avoid looking intermittently at the programme agenda and your wristwatch to confirm when "item seven" will be served.

17. As Much as Possible, Stay Till the End

Don't be in a hurry to rush off before or immediately after the event. It's possible that some people you would love to meet walked in midway into the conference or party. The most appropriate time to connect with them is when the event comes to an end.

Chapter 14

How to win
the mindshare of people

"You must win the mindshare
before the market share."
– BETH COMSTOCK

In networking, affinity is simply a natural liking for, or attraction to a person, for which such a natural fondness or pull is felt. If you get along with someone very well, you have an affinity with him or her. I have heard people ask me, "How do I win others over to my side?" or "How do I win the mindshare of others?" How do I make people like me?" Here are some tips to consider:

1. **Find common grounds.** Finding common ground is a technique for facilitating interpersonal relationships. Rather than focus on things that you differ on, when you are with people highlight and concentrate on the things that you both agree on. What you focus on expands; and once your mind illuminates it through your thought process, it will reflect on your attitude and actions. Superior networkers look out for points of congruence, not points of departure.

2. **Make simple points that everybody agrees on.** When you are having a discussion with a group of people, try as much as possible to always highlight the points of others that you agree with before stating your own position.

3. **Address people by their names when you are having a conversation.** We all like the sound of our names. Especially if you call the name the way the name was introduced to you. People do a lot to 'jazz up' their names. So, Patricia becomes Pat; then later becomes Tricia, before transforming to Trich; and would probably end up as Cia. During discussions or conversation, mention people's names intermittently. Say things like, "You see Chuks eh... my view is..." Tricia, I was thinking..." Addressing people by their names creates rapport and personalizes the relationship.

4. **Acknowledge points made by others.** The rule according the Stephen Covey is to seek first to understand before seeking to be understood. You may not agree with the other person's position,

but you must agree with their rights to hold their positions. Let people know that you listened and heard them. Paraphrase what they said before stating your position, especially if you disagree with them. Say something like, "what I hear you say madam is that...Well I appreciate your perspective on this... However, this is what I think or how I see it..." Show understanding of the views of others.

5. **Focus on the issue, not on the people**. When you have a disagreement with people, focus on the issues rather than the people. Whenever you find a conflict or disagreement between people, there are usually four variables at play. The variables are: the people involved, the issues involved, the facts of the matter and resolution strategies. If one, or both parties focus more on the personality differences rather than the issues or facts as well as resolution options, that matter inevitably, becomes intractable. So, if you want to create better affinity with people, always focus on the issues rather than the person involved.

6. **Speak the language people understand**. Cultural humility is a critical rapport-building trait. You are more likely to win people over to your side when you sincerely look at the world from their glasses. Speak to their hearts not just to their heads. If your position appears to you to be so simple, logical and easy to understand, yet the other party can't seem to understand you, perhaps you are the problem and not the other party. You haven't said it the way they will understand.

Have you ever asked your driver or messenger to buy you chicken pie and he buys chicken part? Now, who do you think should be blamed for the outcome of this unclear communication? When people don't understand the real message behind your communication, the action they will take based on the miscommunication may create disagreement and tension.

Same thing when you don't fully understand the real import of other people's communication. To create affinity therefore, it is important that you confirm that the other party fully understands you and your message. Conversely, you should seek clarity when you have doubts in your communication with others.

Chapter 15

How to
Manage Contact Information

"The richest people in the world look for and build
networks; everyone else looks for work..."
Robert Kiyosaki

What do you do with all the call cards you get at the networking events you attend? What do you do with the notes you took during your conversation with people? How do you manage contact information so that following-up and following-through will be easy?

I have identified ten steps.... take in a sequential order.

STEP 1:

Gather and collate all the call cards and contact details you harvested during networking. You can do this daily or weekly depending on the frequency of your networking, and the number of business cards or volume of contact information you generate.

STEP 2:

Create a database, preferably an electronic database. A database is simply a mass of data in a computer, arranged for rapid expansion, updating, and retrieval. A retrievable database helps to quickly call up the information you need about your contacts. Examples of electronic, retrievable database packages are: Excel, Outlook, Oracle, FileMaker Pro, Microsoft Access, Microsoft SQL Server, SAP, MySQL and database management system or DBMS.

The database should have two sections. The first section is where you store the personal contact information of the people you meet. This section should contain the following fields: Name of the contact, Title (Mr., Mrs., Chief, Doctor, Alhaji, etc.), Home address, Telephone number, Private email address, Point of contact (which is where you met the person), Expandable notes section (this is where you input information about some personal things they shared with you or the notes your took when you met.

For instance, if someone mentioned during your interaction that his daughter would be wedding on a particular date or that he plans to relocate his family, note the information in the expandable notes section. This information may come in handy as a good conversational opener when you want to follow-up.)

The second section of the database is where you store the Professional contact details. The information in this section should include: Name of organization, Designation (Managing Director, Vice President, Marketing Manager, etc.), Office address, Telephone numbers, Official email address, Website and Expandable notes section.

However, the expandable notes section for the professional element of the database should contain information you gathered about people's business. For instance, their plans of opening new branches, changing line of business, changing jobs, etc.

STEP 3:
Categorize your contacts: You can use demographic categorization such as (age, gender, education, tribe, income and religion). You can also use Psychographic categorization such as (lifestyle, attitude, personal values, social class or status). Geographic categorization looks at elements like (their city, area, state). You can also categorize them into industry, vocation or profession.

STEP 4:
Code contacts into level of importance and relevance to your legacy, career, family, and financial goals. What you are doing here is to identify the ones that you consider more relevant than others in specific areas of your life. So, you can choose the ones you think are important to your humanitarian or charity goals, choose the ones relevant to your legacy goals, financial goals, spiritual aspirations, career pursuits etc.

STEP 5:
Decide which people you will focus on and reconnect with.

STEP 6:
Do a background check about them and their business.

STEP 7:
Check your database to see if there are people in your network that might know the ones you just met.

STEP 8:
Create an action plan for follow-up The action plan should include: what you are going to do to follow up, and when you are going to follow up; who you will see and when you will see the people; who you will call and when you will call the people; who you will write and when you will write.

STEP 9:
Decide what you will do for the different categories of your contacts to add value and enshrine you in their consciousness.

STEP 10:
Diarize appointments for next meeting.

◆◆◆

HOW TO FOLLOW-UP AND KEEP IN TOUCH
AFTER MEETING SOMEONE

So you have initiated the conversation with people, introduced yourself, sustained the conversation, joined other people's conversation, exchanged contact details and you are now back to your base. For most people, that is the end of the networking activity.

Invariably, these are the people who don't benefit from networking and who go on to complain that networking doesn't work. All you have done so far is just contact initiation. It's more like greet and meet. It is without doubt an important step in business and social networking. But it's just the foundation.

It's amazing how we sometimes do all the right things in making contacts and establishing basic relationships and then quickly loose the contacts because we don't keep in touch. We can easily get carried away by other commitments as well as the pursuit for new contacts that we lose touch of the ones that we already have.

Sometimes, this comes back to haunt us when we suddenly realize that we need some of these people to refer us to somebody, give us information or provide counsel.

Keeping the line of communication open is the oil that lubricates the connection. How do you keep in touch so your contacts so don't forget you? Here are some tips:

I. Call, send a text message or do an email to the people you met as soon as possible (same day evening if the meeting was in the morning or the following day if you met in the evening). In making the call, sending the text message or email it is important that you follow these steps.

(a) Identify yourself.

(b) State where you met the person.

(c). Say it was a pleasure meeting them and finally confirm that they got back to their base safely, etc.

For example, you call the person and he picks and then you go, "Hello, good evening madam. This is Ferdinand, Ferdinand Ibezim. We met at the conference on autism yesterday. It was indeed a pleasure meeting you. I thoroughly enjoyed the perspective you shared on dealing with hyperactivity. Hope you got back safely? Thank you."

2. Follow through to provide anything you had promised as quickly as possible.

3. Use your calendar and diary creatively. Mark important dates in your calendar and diarize important appointments.

4. Use electronic prompters to remind you way ahead of events so you don't forget.

5. Watch out for opportunities to keep in touch. Some of the opportunities would include:

   ▶ On their birthdays or anniversaries.
   ▶ Important community events.
   ▶ If you see an article about them or their companies in the newspapers.
   ▶ If you see them or hear the names of business mentioned in the radio or television.
   ▶ If you hear of, or you are invited to a conference that you think they might be interested in.
   ▶ If you hear they have received an award, promoted or recognised.
   ▶ You see or hear of a business opportunity you think might benefit them.
   ▶ You meet someone you would like to introduce to them.

6. Observe personal or organizational changes. If for instance you hear that your contact is moving from one company to another or that he is opening a new branch somewhere, call him or send a text message wishing him well.

7. Report any changes in your situation. If you are relocating, changing jobs, getting married, going back to school, etc. mention it to your contacts.

8. Where applicable, visit them occasionally.

9. Use what we call clip and ship to keep in touch. If you see any article in the newspapers that you think might be of interest to

your contacts, cut off that portion of the article, write a note on your business card, staple your business card on the article and send to your contact.

If you also come across any book of interest, buy it, staple your business card on the book and ship to your contact. The note on your business card should read, "Good day madam, I just seen this article in the Harvard Business Review and I think you would find it useful. Regards" or "Hello Sir, I saw this book in a bookshop. I went through the table of contents and feel strongly that you might find the chapter on penetrating Asian markets relevant to your export business. Regards."

10. The tenth way of keeping in touch with your contacts is by attending their events. If she is celebrating her anniversary, giving out the daughter in marriage or just having a party, be there. And when you get there, make sure you are noticed in a nice way.

11. Invest in a robust contact management system. A contact manager according to Wikipedia is a software program that enables users to easily store and find contact information, such as names, addresses and telephone numbers. They are contact-centric databases that provide a fully integrated approach to tracking of all information and communication activities linked to contacts. A contact management system (CMS) provide the following advantages:

▸ Centralized repository of contact information
▸ Ready to use database with searching
▸ Email integration
▸ Scheduling of appointments and meetings
▸ Document management
▸ Notes and conversation management
▸ Customizable fields

12. Use your referrals and mutual friends to keep in touch. You do this by asking your friends to mention to your other friends that you always ask after them.

13. Use the 1/12/50 Rule for Connecting to Contacts. This is a simple principle that you can apply to continually connect to people in your network.

   In the 1/12/50 Rule represents the actions that would take place either the first day of the week, the first week of the month or the first month of the year. You should ask yourself, "What are the things I need to do on the first day of every week? What are the things I need to do the first week of every month, and the first month of every year to continually connect with the people in my network?"

   It is also important that you divide people in your database into categories. You can then say, 'I'll send text messages every Monday to my category A contacts. I'll send emails every Monday to those in category B'. The e-mails you send should be creative and relevant to the people in your network. You can also say that, 'Every first week of the month, I'll do clip and ship for those in category A of my network.' You can even choose to send gifts to certain people among your category A contacts every first week of the month.

The 12 in the rule represents doing what you choose to do consistently over the next 12 weeks or months, so it becomes a predictable pattern. People in your network can now expect a certain kind of SMS, a certain kind of email, certain kind of gifts, certain kind of information from you at a particular point in time. It positions you positively in their frame of consciousness.

The **50** in the rule represent my challenge for you. I challenge you to keep in touch with a minimum of 50 people in your contact every month if you are new in networking; or every day/week if you are an experienced networker. You can keep in touch virtually by emails or text messages. You can also keep in touch kinetically by physical visits, telephone calls or by sending gifts.

> THINK ON THESE
>
> **Meanwhile, the most important way to stay and keep in touch is to… keep and stay in touch.**

Chapter 16

Making requests from people in your network

"First, you have to be visible in the community. You have to get out there and connect with people. It's not net-sitting or net-eating. It is called networking; you have to work at it"
– DR. IVAN MISNER

In the chapter on how to conduct yourself when you join a group or an association for networking, we had advised you not to make unreasonable demands from people in your network. Does that mean that making requests is a taboo in networking? Absolutely not! As a matter of fact, making requests is a fundamental and important element of business and social networking. Making requests not only helps you get what you want in life, it also helps you build relationships with others; as well as helps you to expand your network.

It is amazing that some networkers don't ask for what they want from others; and yet they complain that networking is not rewarding. How can you receive when you have not asked? How can you find when you have not sought? How can the doors of opportunities be opened to you when you have not knocked on them? You can, and you should make requests from members of your network. You should also expect other people to make requests and ask for favours from you.

So, why don't people make requests in networking? Why don't people make requests

There are so many reasons why people don't make requests in networking and in life generally. As we highlight the reasons, you would notice that most of them exist in the mind and are merely assumptions.

1. Fear of Rejection

"What if she says no?" they ask. I am sure you have heard that F.E.A.R simply means: Fantasized Experiences Appearing Real. "What if she says no?" is just that - fantasy. The rejection that you fear only exists in the realm of your fantasy. You have not asked, so how do you know you would be rejected?

By the way, what would you lose if ask and you don't get? You don't have what you want to ask for in the first place. So if you ask and you don't get, you have not lost anything, because you didn't have anything. As a matter of fact, the real risk is in not asking. Because by not asking, you are losing the chances and possibilities of getting what you want if you ask.

2. Fear of Embarrassment

The second reason why people don't make requests is, "I don't want to be embarrassed". Fear of embarrassment is actually a symptom of low self-esteem. Nothing is an embarrassment until you interpret it to be so. Develop and make self-validating confessions and declarations whenever things or people appear to embarrass you. When people say no to your requests, they have not said no to you. They have only said no to your request. I will be dealing with how to handle rejection and embarrassment later in the book.

3. Waiting for the Right Time

The third reason why people don't make request is, "Is it not too early or too soon for me to make a request?" We agree with you that timing is critical in making requests. However, timing is not necessarily a function of how long you have met or known somebody. You can meet someone today and in the course of casual conversation something is said or an opportunity presents itself for you to make a request.

For instance, you can meet someone in the aircraft, initiate a conversation, introduce yourself and in the course of the conversation he mentions that he has been having challenges finding the right candidate to fill a vacant position in his company. Now, if you have a younger sister or know someone that fits the profile he's looking for, you can politely say so, and ask if you may send your sister to him for a chat.

4. The Plate is Full

"I am sure he has a lot on his plate." is another assumption that people make. It's good to be considerate in deciding who and when to make a request. But again, you are just assuming that the person's plate is full. What if he just cleared the plate? Is it not possible that every other person is thinking like you are thinking, and therefore his plate is actually empty?

5. Status Fright

The fifth assumption is, "She's not in the same league or class with me." This statement can be a sign of inferiority complex or superiority complex. Amazingly, there are people who would not make requests to people lower than them in strata, education, wealth, etc. For such people it is condescending to do so. For others, making requests to those older, richer, more educated or more powerful than them is "hanging your clothes where you cannot stretch to retrieve it". That's inferiority complex and it's a success destroyer.

6. I Don't Want to Be a Parasite

The sixth reason why people don't make requests is that they think it is parasitic to do so. For those with this mindset, there position is that it is only fair to make requests to those that you can also help. My question is, 'How do you know for sure that they do not need you now or that they would not need you in the future?' In any case, there is no rule that states that only those you can help should help you.

7. Labeling

"People are arrogant, selfish and proud" is another mental block to making requests. It's called labeling; sometimes driven by fallacy of over generalization. The fact that one person of a particular demography, geography and psychography has behaved in a certain way does not mean that everybody fitting the same description will behave likewise.

8. Nothing Until I Am Certain

"I don't want to waste my time on something I am not sure of." is the eight mental block stopping people from making requests. Can you really be sure of anything? Can you be sure of the next minute? Can you be sure that you when you leave your house to work, school or business that you will return home alive and well? So why do you step out? You step out despite the risks because your focus is on the rewards of leaving your house. Adopt the same attitude in making requests. Take the risk. Focus on the joy of getting what you want.

9. No Intimate Relationship Yet

"They don't know me well enough, and I don't know them well enough." Well, when would be well enough? Can the request wait? Will they still be available when you know them well enough? What if other people cease the opportunity before you are ready?

10. I Don't Want to Take Advantage of People

The final reason is the assumption that, "They would think I am taking advantage of them". My response to this assumption is, "don't ask them because you want to take advantage of them". If your motive is right and your conscience is clear, you shouldn't bother so much about what people would think or do. You can't really determine what someone would think or do; can you?

HOW TO MAKE REQUESTS
FROM PEOPLE IN YOUR NETWORK

Having dealt with the mental blocks and assumptions, how do you now proceed to make the request? How should you make requests to people in your network? Like most things in the science and art of networking, there are steps, guidelines and rules for making requests.

Step 1: Decide on the Request

The first step is to decide exactly what requests you want to make. Our advice is that you revisit the networking goals you set when you were making your networking plans – remember your legacy goals, spiritual goals, financial goals, career goals and family goals? What do you need from individuals or groups to achieve these goals? For your career goals for instance what requests would you need to make to fast track the achievement of the goal? So the first step is to dimension the requests you want to make in the various aspects of your life.

Step 2: Map out Your Network

The second step is to map out your network or members of the associations you belong, to identify the people you would consider making requests to.

Step 3: Rank

Use your own criteria to rank or weight them. You can have the 'A group' being the ones who have the entire key qualifying elements. This may include: approachability, capacity, willingness, relevance.

Step 4: Earn Trust and Confidence

Decide what steps or actions to take to earn the trust and confidence of the people you plan to present your request to. How would you make them buy into your vision and see that granting you the request is worthwhile?

Step 5: Do You Want to Use a Referral?

Decide if you need a referral to introduce you to them. So, if you want to make a request to somebody, you may wish to use people who are close to him or her.

Step 6: List Your Requests

Write down the all requests you want to make in no particular order. Just imagine that you have a blank cheque and that you can get all that you want if you ask.

Step 7: Analyze and Prioritize Your Requests

You can use the ABCDE method to prioritize your request. (A), being the things you must have; (B), being the things you would like to have; (C), being the things that would be nice to have; (D), the things you can delegate to others outside of your network to handle and E being the things on your list you should eliminate.

Step 8: Decide How You Are Going to Make the Request.

Would be it verbal during a face-to-face meeting or in written form? Would be by telephone call, text message or email?

Step 9: Decide the Timing

Decide when you are going to make the request.

Step 10: Make the request

CRITICAL SUCCESS FACTORS IN GETTING
THE REQUEST RIGHT

I.   There Should Be No Ambiguity about What You Are Asking for
State your needs and wants clearly in such a way that others will understand them. Don't rigmarole. Don't dance about it. Don't imply it. Just make the request directly and in simple terms. If you want my pen, ask for the pen. Don't start by telling me stories of how the pen was invented and how that everybody should always have one. But somehow you don't have one; and then expect me to deduce that you need a pen.

2.   Make Your Request Comprehensive
If you want the car and my driver, as well as money for fuel, say so at once. Don't make piece meal requests. People would think you are playing smart and manipulating them if they grant you the first

request and you now make another request.

3. Be Specific
State exactly what you want, how you want it and when you want it. That way, the other person can easily process your request to determine if your request can be granted or not.

4. Don't Overload Your Request with Too Many Details
This is particularly important when making written requests. Just give information sufficient for the other person to process your request.

5. Be Ready to Answer the Question, "Why Me"?
If the person you are making the request to asks you, "why did you come to me and not to other people who have more capacity to help you?" Be ready to answer that question. Let people know why you are approaching them and not others. Talk about their pedigree, position, statements, competence or attitude that attracted you to them.

6. Don't Create Window or Excuses for the Other Person to Decline Your Request

For instance don't say, "I will like you to write the forward for my new book...but I will understand if your schedule is too tight to accommodate my request". You are already giving that person a window of excuse.

7. Don't Appear Beggarly
Be humble when you are making requests, but don't be timid. Be strong. Show self-confidence. Don't start your request by telling what a pathetic and helpless state you are in, or complaining about how the world has been conspiring to keep you down.

8. Don't Be Sorry for Asking
Don't say things like, "Let me start by apologizing if my request will

upset you." "I am sorry to bother you, but..."

9. Don't Adulate

Don't make it look as if the other person is a messiah without whom you will perish. People interpret that as being patronizing.

10. Reverse the Role

Put yourself in the other person's shoes. Ask yourself, "If I were in this person's position, how would I like to be approached".

11. Be Assertive in Your Request

That means that should sell how helping you will add value to a higher cause. For instance, if you want someone to be your guarantor for a business loan, show how getting that loan will improve your business and help you add value to others and society.

12. There Should Be No Pretenses

If you need something urgently, make your request in a way that communicates the urgency. Don't ask as if you were not in a hurry to get it. On the other hand, don't paint a picture of urgency when the request can wait for a while.

13. Don't Become a Nuisance

When you ask, don't pester. Give others time to process your request. Don't put people under unnecessary pressure with irritating text messages, constant reminders, phone calls, visits, etc.

14. Don't Create Confusion

When you have made a request, don't confuse the other person with another request that will make him/her forget the first request.

15. Believe

When you make requests believe that your request will be granted. Don't ask with any fear or doubt in your mind. And don't go around thinking or believing that your requests will not be granted. When people make you promises, believe they would honour their commitments.

●●●

HOW TO HANDLE REJECTION OF YOUR REQUESTS

You can't get everything you want, even if you ask. As a networker, you are going to meet so many roadblocks, hear so many 'nos' and a lot of your requests will be declined. Your part as networker is to handle the declined requests in a way that it becomes a stepping-stone to a higher level, and not an energy sapper that leads to despair and frustration.

So, what should you do when your requests are not granted; when you ask and you don't receive; when you knock and the door is not opened and when you seek and you don't find?

1. *Don't Take It Personal*

Remember that you are not the one that has been rejected. A "no' is not a rejection of you. A declined request is not a final seal on access. There is nothing wrong in making more than one request to the same person, as long as you follow the guidelines listed in *"How to make Request"*. In addition, there is no rule that states that you cannot make the same request to another person in your network; even if they know themselves.

It is your request that has been rejected. You name has not changed. Your age, status, qualification, height, competence, dreams, goals and destiny have not changed.

Remember that you have not lost anything by asking and not receiving. You didn't have what you asked for before asking. Now you don't have it. The worst that could have happened is that you have returned to the status quo. In actual fact though, you have not returned to the status quo. You have actually improved. You have learnt some lessons.

2. *Identify Reasons for the Declined Request*
Dimension what you asked for, how you asked, when you asked and whom you asked to locate the reason for the negative response.

3. *Identify Lessons*
List the lessons for asking and not receiving. Note the positive and negative lessons.

4. *Understand What No Actually Means*

- What did the "no" mean?
- Was it a timing issue (I asked at the wrong time)?
- Was it a resource issue (the other person didn't have the resources I requested)?
- Was it a capacity issue?
- Was it a position issue (the person didn't have the authority to grant my request)?

5. *Identify Your B. A. D. R.*

- What is your best alternative to this declined request?
- What other options can you explore?
- Who else can you approach with this request?

6. *How Can You Use This Encounter to Strengthen the Relationship?*
How do I ensure that my relationship with the other person is not damaged, but rather strengthened by this interaction?

7. *Prepare for the next request.*

HOW TO DECLINE REQUESTS FROM OTHERS

Having looked at how to handle a no, or a declined request from others, let's now turn our attention to how to say no to a requests from others. As a networker you are going to face so many situations where people, including those you respect, love or defer to are going to ask you for things or make requests that you would not be able or willing to grant or accede to.

Saying no is part of the communication options in a relationship. The problem is not really with saying no; as much as it is in the way, manner and time you say no. The fundamental and critical thing is that saying no should not damage or affect your relationships negatively.

Once you understand the request and decide you want to say no, choose the kind of no that best suits the person and situation.

HERE ARE SOME GENERAL RULES TO FOLLOW:

1. You can say no, **firmly** and **calmly**, without feeling sorry for yourself. You don't have to feel guilty that you are saying no to a request you know you cannot grant.

2. You can say no, followed by a **straightforward explanation** of what you are feeling or what you are willing not to do. Examples: "I'm uncomfortable doing that," "No, I'm not willing to do that," "No, I don't want to do that, "No, I don't like to do that."

3. You can say no, and then **give a choice**, such as: "I don't have time today, but I could help out the first thing tomorrow morning." Or, "Not now; however, I will when I get this done, which could be in an hour."

4. You can say no, and then **give an alternative** or refer to the person making request to another person, such as, "You may wish

to visit this website to get help" or "Have you approached the Peniel Foundation to assist you?"

5. Say no, and then **clarify your reasons**. This does not include long-winded statements filled with excuses, justifications, and rationalizations. It's enough that you do not want to say yes. Your clarification should only be given to provide the receiver more information so that he or she can better understand your position.

6. You can make an **empathetic listening statement**, then say no. You may paraphrase the content and feeling of the request, and then state your no. Example: "I know how important it is for you to do your industrial attachment in my office because of the experience it will offer you. However, we have filled all the available vacancies for such positions"

7. You can say yes, and then **give your reasons for not doing** it or your alternative solution. This approach is very interesting. You may want to use it in situations when you are willing to meet the request, but not at the time or in the way the other person wants it. For example: "I will be willing to give you my car to use, but it won't be tomorrow that you are asking for" or "It will my pleasure to review your project, but I won't be available till next month"

8. Select a concise, one-sentence statement and **repeat** it no matter what the other person says or does. Examples: "I understand how you feel, but I'm not willing...."; "I'm not interested..."; "I don't want to...'; "I'm uncomfortable doing that, so I don't want to..."; "You might be right, but I'm not interested."

After each statement by the other person, say your persistent response sentence. It's important that you don't get sidetracked by responding to any issue the other person brings up. Just keep saying your one liner no.

9.   Use **your natural no.** You may have developed your own style of saying no based on your past experience and personality. If so, use it. But remember the golden rule. However you say the no, it must not damage the relationship.

HOW TO GIVE AND RECEIVE FEEDBACK

Networking is primarily an interaction between people for the main purpose of nurturing and building long-term and mutually rewarding relationships. The oil that lubricates the engine of networking is communication. And communication is mainly a process of giving and receiving back.

In this section, we shall examine some of the critical underpinnings and success factors in giving and receiving feedback during networking. Let's start with giving feedback

GIVING FEEDBACK

1.   In giving feedback, make the feedback **specific.** Don't bit about the bush. Say exactly what you want to say? If for instance you want to decline a request, say so. If you want offer explanations for declining do so without any rigmarole.

2.   Your feedback should be **timely.** If there are issues or concerns you feel you should talk about with someone in your network, bring up the matter while it is fresh. Don't wait to link the feedback with another matter in the future. You will come across as harboring malice.

3.   **Own** the feedback that you give. Don't give feedback in a way that suggests that you are not certain of what you are saying or that the consequences of the feedback should be borne by a third party. There is a difference between seeking clarification and giving feedback. If you want to give feedback you should

own the feedback.

4. Feedback should be **sincere**.

5. Your feedback should be **balanced**. Even if you want to give someone a negative feedback, deliberately look for something nice also to say. Preferably, start with the positive feedback before giving negative feedback.

6. Give the other person time to **respond** to your feedback. When you give feedback, give the other party time to respond to your feedback.

7. **Listen** to the response of your feedback with an open and unbiased mind.

8. If you are giving negative feedback about the other person's behavior, dressing or attitude it will be great to offer **suggestions** on ways to improve or change.

HOW TO RECEIVE FEEDBACK

Let's now turn our attention on how to receive feedback.

1. **Listen actively** to the feedback given. Don't just listen to the words. Listen to the emotions, pace, tone, pitch and volume behind the voice. Watch out for the things not said, but implied.

2. Beware of your **attitude.** Be careful of what is going through your mind when you are listening to feedback. Don't allow filters distract you.

3. **Control** your emotion. Don't get too excited and don't get angry. Either of these emotions can make you lose the real import of the feedback being given.

4. Be **open** to feedback. Let people know that you are willing and ready to receive feedback. You will lose a lot of counsel and direction if you come across as someone who abhours feedback.

5. Don't be too **defensive.** You should take feedback as a call to improve and not an attack on your dignity or an interrogation of your competence.

6. Understand the **needs, interests and goals** of the person giving

you the feedback. What does this person really need from me? What are her obvious and not too obvious interests in this matter, and what goals are being pursued? What would I benefit if I accept the feedback and what would I lose if I reject the feedback?

7. Understand the **message** clearly. What outcome would prove that you understood the feedback? What are you being asked to do? When are you expected to do it? How are you going to do it?

8. Seek clarifications and **ask questions**. Even when you think that you have fully comprehended the feedback, still ask questions. It is better to ask a stupid question than to make a costly mistake.

9. **Paraphrase** what you heard to confirm understanding. Summarize the major elements of the feedback in your own words.

10. **Analyze**, reflect and decide what you would do with the feedback.

11. **Thank** the person for giving you the feedback.

12. Take **action** based on the feedback.

Chapter 17

How to manage
your relationships effectively

"It's all about people. It's about
networking and being nice to
people and burning any bridges."
– MIKE DAVIDSON

I n this concluding part of our discourse on networking, it is expedient to examine the nitty-gritty of effective management of relationships.

> You may have great people and wonderful communication skills at your disposal, but if you don't have the discipline to follow through, you won't have great results.

I consider this chapter vital to your networking success. It would be a sheer waste of effort and time digging deep for contacts and then failing to explore the massive possibilities they represent. The ability to follow up on your networking contacts - or follow through on your networking efforts - would go a long way in yielding super results for you.

We have been handed the opportunity of connecting to people who may be the door to great opportunities. Nonetheless, those opportunities would remain latent if we do not go beyond the point of acquaintanceship to following through with the prospects and clients until the desired objective is accomplished.

In my knowledge transfer sessions, I usually instruct fresh networkers to treat relationships with utmost care: "Handle contacts the same way doctors handle the case files of their patients." You need to open a personal file for everyone you meet. The file may be electronic or paper-based. You may also use your mobile phone for this purpose, depending on how sophisticated it is. If you choose to use your mobile phone, ensure that you synchronize the data as often as you can with those on your computer to have an up to date database and backup.

I am often amused when I hear some networkers pick a call and exclaim, "Oh! I didn't realise it's you! I lost my phone three weeks ago and all my contact numbers are gone." This is simply shameful. You must create a backup system to avoid the regret arising from such. It is not only an easy task, it is also very expedient. Your first rule should be to guard your contacts' information. Protect them; treat them like they are the pillars of your business structure, because they really are.

When you decide to treat your contacts in this manner, one of two things will happen: you will either be amazed at the huge number of contacts you have made or embarrassed at the slim database you have only been able to put together in the past, say, six months. Creating a tangible or electronic filing system for your contacts would also help you to know the actual number of prospects/clients you have in select industries and sectors.

> I once worked with a marketer on a monthly marketing follow-up routine. We did a lot of follow-ups one day and met some new prospects with whom we exchanged cards. The following day, I asked the same marketer to give me the mobile number of a particular banker we had met the previous day. Surprisingly, she said said, "Sorry, Sir. I don't have it saved on my phone and his card is at home."

I told her pointblank that I was not happy she was operating at such mediocre level. I had expected that she would have saved the numbers right there, or when she got to the office, and send the banker an SMS afterward to thank him for his time or even request for a proper appointment. She did not. She almost buried the opportunity, and would have probably misplaced the cards, but for my query.

You must be alert to opportunities that expose you to greater responsibilities and connect you to people.

Conversations are critical in networking as they hold the key to future dealings with people. You can discern people's wants or needs from conversing with them, enabling you to meet their desires Conversations therefore provide opportunities for actions and consequent results.

Many people set out to network but end up not really networking. They meet people, no doubt, but do not go beyond the first meeting. Networking does not end when you are through talking with a contact. It is a means to an end. Once you are done, the details of the person you have been conversing with should go into your database file immediately for assessment and consideration of your next line of action. A secondary filing system should also be in place to create a chain of other referrals you may have built through a single contact.

Having a secondary file would help you know how well you have built on each contact. Your filing system should be as creative as possible. For instance, you should create queries of how well you have related with the client, your next appointment, what the highlights of your last meeting were, when you last called the client, when you last sent an email or text, whether you thanked him for the referrals, etc.

A large percentage of networkers plan to get together for lunch, keep in touch with a new prospect or get involved in their industry's associations; but, if they do not follow through, nothing happens. Networking works magic only when you take the necessary action.

Some years ago, I made an unexpected call at the office of one of my mentors. He was happy to see me, as we had not seen each other for some time. I had bought him a book, which I knew would interest him. He was indeed happy to receive it. He gave me advice I would always live to remember. He said, "Ferdinand, you are a young man and you have many years ahead of you. Most young professionals of your time have totally forgotten the key to unlocking opportunities."

I was wondering what he meant by the 'key'. Was it the gift? I certainly did not think the gift was fantastic enough to unlock an opportunity, as I only felt it would be nice to give him something after a long while. He continued, "I appreciate the fact that you have decided to call on me after about nine months since we last saw on that flight to Kaduna. However, young man, do you think you have done well?"

I was stunned at his statement. But before I could respond, he said, "On a scale of one to ten, what do you think you scored in managing our relationship? You stayed for complete nine months without keeping in touch in any way until now. Do you know the number of contacts I have made during that period? Do you know how many referrals I could have given you or the associations I could have recommended to you? My friend, you underperformed. If this is the way you relate with your clients, then you are sabotaging your own networking efforts by the day. And that means you are losing money without knowing!

"You must be on top of managing every contact you make. If you are not committed to building on and managing your relationships, don't even start them. It would be awful to have so many contacts who know next to nothing about you. They don't get any value from you and you expect value from them."

Then he said, "Time and relationship management are critical to success."

My mentor was not sparing in getting his message across. He got me thinking about the magnitude of the blunder I had committed. He concluded by saying,

"Manage your relationships. The reality of the matter is that people only get to think about you in direct proportion to how much you think about and relate with them. If you do not factor people into your thinking, plans and actions, they reciprocate your attitude."

He said although he was not ranked among the top 20 businessmen of his era, he believed he was among the top five relationship managers of his time. He had a custom of keeping in touch with those better than him. He wanted to know what was going on in their lives, how they were doing personally and how their businesses were faring. He needed to be abreast of latest management strategies, business thinking and survival strategies. He maintained a robust database of his contacts and kept in touch with them through calls, letters and personal visits.

He was able to grow his business in a good time because he was in constant contact with those who could help him move faster and the people they referred him to. He also became more organized and lived by the slogan, I say and I do. He arrived at appointment venues 30 minutes early. He never had his client waiting for him after they had agreed on what time to meet and never left a client without requesting a referral. He managed relationships for success.

If you want your ideas to come to fruition, you must effectively combine idea, intention and action. Your ideas and intentions help you determine the most effective actions that will produce the desired results. It's all in the follow-through.

Follow-through is the action you take after making a contact or discovering someone's need. For instance, in one of my knowledge transfer sessions titled Superior Performance in the Workplace, one of the participants said she loves reading management and motivational books and asked if anyone could recommend one. Not quite long after, I ran into Bili Odum, author of the classic **How To Excel At Work–Proven Strategies for Superior Work Performance.** A few days after the workshop, I sent an email to the workshop participant giving her Bili's name, number and email address.

This is following through. The critical part of this aspect of networking is remembering and taking time to provide the needed information or action that brings value.

Follow-through is the next step to take towards entrenching a relationship or creating a valuable result for you or someone else. After acquiring some information, it is up to you to use this information to create value. If you gather a lot of information through your networking but never pass that information along or get back to people, then you are doing the front-end work of networking. The follow-through is what really generates results.

I remember the story of a friend that often ignites some fire in my spirit. A few years ago, he was a young man living a fairly comfortable life. He was an instructor in a consulting firm at Ikeja. He told me how he used to facilitate programmes for his company and the opportunity he had to visit several states in Nigeria. However, he was living from hand to mouth. Paying his bills was an uphill task.

One fateful day, he ran into one of his old friends who told him that one of their mutual friends was doing very well and would be most willing to help him. On hearing this, he became quite hopeful and set out to visit this friend one day. He was shocked at what he saw. His old time friend was now more than comfortable. After spending some time together, as he was about to leave, his friend gave him N100, 000 in cash. He said it was a gift for his wife and new twins.

On his second visit some weeks later, his friend told him, "I want to teach you how to make money. My client is selling off some of his property and is giving out a 10% commission as finder's fee." He thanked him, but pondered what to do to earn the promised commission.

During lunch break at one of his workshops, he mentioned the deal to one of the participants who told him he would introduce him to an uncle who is a big player in the real estate sector and who might go for it. An appointment was fixed and they both went to make a presentation to the old man. That did it. The deal was sealed in less than three weeks. He got a commission from source to the tune of ₦2.5million. This amount may seem small, but it can be huge when lost!

It is painful to note how many of such sums have been lost due to negligence and not following through. If he had caved in to ego and refused to reach out to an old friend or let it stay at the initial ₦100,000 largesse, he wouldn't have clinched that better deal.

Meeting people is easy; it is a natural part of life. You meet people everywhere you go. You connect with some and some are passing acquaintances. Some may turn out to become good friends, clients or associates; while some of the ones you connected with will filter into passing acquaintances because you did not follow through.

As networkers, we must task ourselves continually on our ability to keep the flames of relationships burning. How much of this do we do? You need to appreciate the fact that people are busy and mostly think about their own concerns. It is, therefore, the duty of a networker to get the client thinking about him. What is your game plan for managing your clients for superior results? Nothing changes until we change.

I often send money to my siblings at the end of the month for their upkeep. As their big brother, I consider it my responsibility to offer support in this regard to ease the challenges of our times. However, sometimes, due to personal commitments in other areas, I might be unable to meet up with all their demands. But I have come to realize that the sibling with the best follow- through ability – the one that made more calls, sent more SMS, more reminders and sent appreciation messages for the previous grants he got – often had his request imprinted in my heart more strongly than others. And I often find myself giving him/her top priority in the distribution ratio.

You can see that this example is not far from the reality for today's networking professional. You must be on top of your game. You must make impact in the heart of the client. When the next budget is being drawn, you get firsthand information, and you already know if you need to scale down your proposal. Policies are reviewed for your sake, because you chose to keep in touch and manage relationships.

In networking, seizing the opportunity while the moment is ripe is important. Your duty is to maximize the moment for your benefit. But follow- through can be the decider whether you transform an opportunity into fruition or not.

> **After business meetings, I usually draw up a follow-through plan: I get back to my office, assess the meetings I attended, and I think through the next steps. I draw up an action plan, file the information I may need to refer to in future, send out important emails immediately, and make needful calls; whatever would move my relationships to the next level.**

I remember an embarrassing moment early in my career after a meeting with two top executives in a telecommunication firm. I did not take them seriously. I assumed they were not ready to deal. After the meeting, one of them said, "Please send an electronic copy of your proposal to my box."

I nodded positively. Two weeks later, I had not sent the email. I had totally forgotten about it. I was away, out of town, when I received a call from the prospect. He complained bitterly that I had not sent the mail. He was actually furious because he had recommended my firm as a new consultant to his organization. I pleaded with him to give me 30 minutes to respond. Thankfully, he accepted.

Immediately I dropped the call, it dawned on me that I did not travel with the flash drive that contained the file in question. I became apprehensive. Luckily enough, I had a copy on my system in the office. I called a colleague and asked her to print and send it on my behalf. Follow-through is key to success. If I had been in touch, I would have remembered the e-mail was still pending. If I had noted the requests of the client at the time and reflected on it when I got to the office, I would have acted quickly.

Timing may not be everything, but it certainly can be a critical factor when following up on opportunities. If someone recommends that you call Dangote about a job opportunity and you do not follow through simply because you forgot, misplaced the phone number, put off the call because you did not feel confident then, or got distracted by other things, the position Dangote is hiring for will probably be filled by the time you make that call.

Not all networking efforts, though, will result in positive yields. I have been engaged in networking for several years and I have experienced both fruitful and useless relationships. However, I have come to realize that a relationship that seems unproductive today may turn a goldmine tomorrow. And there's no way of knowing ahead of time which one will become the pot of gold.

Therefore, you must be willing to operate with positive expectancy. You must hope for the best in every relationship. People are a bundle of hidden wealth and it is your duty to tap into their innate resources. This can be accomplished by reaching out to and following through with them in a professional manner.

Just as you cannot expect every prospect to become a client, so also you cannot expect every lead to generate the biggest deal ever. However, you can always be open to the possibility that every person could be a resource. With carefully planned and effective follow-through, you can always go to bed knowing that you have done your part to create an opportunity.

Being the best follow-through networker would put you in front. Numerous benefits would be unfolded to you through effective follow-through. Your perception would soar and more people would be comfortable relating with you. Good follow-through will set you apart from other networkers. By following up promptly on the things that you promise to do, you create a reputation for yourself as a world-class networker.

When you apply follow-through effort, others see you as:

1. Proficient

Proficiency is one important quality a progressive networker must possess. Mediocre networkers are never proficient. They allow situations to dictate their efficiency and effectiveness. When people know they can count on you, you are more attractive to them as a networking partner.

2. Quick to respond

According to Brian Tracy, "One of the qualities of top executives is being brilliant on the basics, having a bias for speed, having a do-it-now attitude and the ability to respond fast to business." Some people, even though they seem to be present, never really respond to what is happening around them. Being responsive shows a level of awareness and alertness.

Your duty is to carefully observe what is going on around you and respond to the situations. When you are reading a magazine and find an article that reminds you of someone, cut and send it to the person concerned right away, with a note on it; that is prompt follow-through. Follow-through involves being responsive and taking action based on what you observe. If you are not conscious of what is going on around you, you will not even know what action to take.

3. Organized

This is a key quality of top networkers. A disorganized networker would only get embarrassed at critical turnaround moments. You cannot succeed as a professional networker if you lead a disorganized life style. If you are not organized, the chances of something falling through the cracks are multiplied.

Ensure you have a designated place where you can always find that name and phone number. Know where to put that reminder to call someone. Keep note cards, stamps, stationery, business cards and other supplies handy to make it easy for you to follow-up on people.

4. Courteous

On a scale of one to ten, how would you rate your courtesy quotient? It is sad that many networkers do not relate courtesy with their success potential. Networkers who have courteous dispositions attract more people and businesses. It is courteous to get back to people when you promised and to promptly thank them after they have done something for you.

TECHNIQUES FOR EFFECTIVE FOLLOW-THROUGH

The following simple techniques would help you to follow through effectively:

■ **Take immediate follow-through action:** Cultivate the habit of quick and immediate follow through. Do not leave anything to chance.

■ **Make a follow-up phone call:** Never be scared of making a call to your contact. Time the call. Plan the call so that you convey the information you have in an intelligent and courteous manner. But, most importantly, make the call; make it quickly and move the relationship forward.

■ **Send an email message:** An email to a contact can produce tremendous results. You can compose an email that would articulately convey the key points of your intent. Always include valuable information that would portray you as an intelligent professional and also proffer researched business information that would add value to their business. If the contact had earlier asked for some information, ensure that the email captures it.

■ **Send letters as part of follow-through:** Use letters to help contacts remember the key points of your last meeting. Send thank-you letters while reiterating the next steps that would lead to a mutually beneficial relationship. Most importantly, send the letter on time.

■ **Maintain your network by staying in touch:** This cannot be overemphasized. You must stay in touch to keep abreast with market trends and opportunities that would be available only to someone who is in touch.

- **Be as good as your word:** As we have learnt from certain past leaders, "let your nay be nay and your yea be yea." This is the best way to brand yourself as a dependable professional.

ON MARBLE

When we're together or when we're apart, you're first in my thoughts and first in my heart.
– AUTHOR UNKNOWN

Chapter 18

How To Use The Social Media For Networking

"Primarily because of the power of the Internet, people of modest means can band together and amass vast sums of money that can change the world for some public good if they all agree"
– WILLIAM J. CLINTON."

Whenhen was the last time you were on the Internet? Was it for a social or business reason? There is no denying the fact. No hiding from the new reality before us. The Internet, and all the technologies it has generated, has revolutionized our lives forever.

Networking is now significantly much easier and wider. Distance, time and other barriers are no longer hindrances to achieving your goal in life. Many different platforms and possibilities exist out there. You can meet the greatest experts in any field, and develop useful resources and relationships using the Internet.

The many social and business websites make it possible for anyone with Internet access in the remotest or most obscure corner of the globe to network and meet people who could facilitate the realisation of one's aspiration. Online networking has mitigated the restraints of physical networking; thus making networking an even more accessible pastime.

We are all part of a world evolving into a global society with fluid, overlapping, national and geographic boundaries. Business processes are now initiated quicker. The Internet makes real-time access to key information and prompt decision-making very possible.

The Internet also presents you the opportunity to network with people of similar or related vocational and professional interests. Social networking websites are now the most popular platforms for networking. You are no longer restricted to physically attending conferences and other social events. You can participate in many desired activities on diverse platforms from the proximity of your computer or mobile telephone. You can interact on social websites and attend webinars (web seminars) alongside businesspersons, artistes, and others of interest to you around the world.

The Internet presents you a source of massive opportunities regardless of your profession or industry. There are resources to meet needs as diverse as getting a new job, consulting services, business/service collaborations and online marketing campaigns. Other important benefits include sourcing for funds, scientific and medical collaborations, and even starting a business from the scratch!

Now, why should you extend your networking activities to the Internet? Let me show you the huge potential abounding in the Internet with the following statistics:

- There are estimated 3.3 billion internet users globally
- It is widely reported that there are about 86.2 million Internet users in Nigeria.
- There are 1.49 billion Facebook users worldwide. WhatsApp (500 million), Twitter (284 million) and Instagram (200 million)
- According to Tech Cabal, there are about 16 million active Facebook users in Nigeria.

The question is, how do you begin? Where does online networking begin? Simple! You can start from where you are, from whom you know. Begin with your offline contacts, friends and colleagues. Use the search function on the website if you need to retrieve an email or web address from a name you already know. You can then go on to adding them as friends, connecting with or following them.

Another option would be to import your email contact list and then send invitations to your contacts so that they can connect with you.

Communication devices these days are enabled to help you network better online. From the average mobile phone, iPad, laptop, and desktop computers. Nowadays, the question "What is your BB PIN, What is your WhatsApp number or Twitter handle?" is exchanged among many young people meeting for the first time. If you own a smart phone, you have a social pool you can use for networking. You can also use Skype Google Talk and WhatsApp, amongst others to make phone calls and video calls over the Internet.

Are you averse to technology? Be assured you do not have to be an IT guru to use these online resources. All you need is an open mind and a willingness to explore. Older and more conservative folks may be a little reluctant to explore these online platforms. However, to break the ice, let me ask, 'Do you email?' If your answer is yes, then you have already crossed the first hurdle.

You already have an online presence. Now, you need to make your online identity more interactive. My advice: begin from one of the popular websites.

For the corporate professional, I would suggest *Facebook* or *LinkedIn*.

THE PLATFORMS

There are diverse online platforms for friendship, education, business, vocational, and political persuasions. The spheres of work and play constantly overlap. I will run through an extensive list of the most prevalent types here. However, I will spend more time explaining the features and benefits of Social Network Services and Blogs. These have a more direct bearing on the type of networking we are discussing.

First is the **Online chat rooms** which date back from the early days of online networking. Prominent sites offering this service include Yahoo and MSN. They are usually themed on an interest or subject area. Thus, there are chat rooms for enthusiasts of dating, culture, technology, astrology, and so on. Visitors to these chat rooms have reduced over the years. The instant messaging feature of this service has been adapted to a more streamlined service within a user's email inbox. Instant messages are quicker and more interactive than emails.

Next are the websites known as virtual worlds, like **Second Life**. These sites give the user a complete alternate life with avatars or 3D images representing the user. They are websites for meeting people, and sharing knowledge and resources.

These two have their own uses worldwide as avenues for social interaction. However, I will focus on the most popular networking platforms, explaining their features and the many benefits they offer.

SOCIAL NETWORK SERVICES

Facebook.com

The most popular of the platforms is Facebook. I am certain that this is no news to you. Facebook has about one 1.4 billion registered users – 16 million of them in Nigeria; and over 120 million across Africa. Over 1 billion users access Facebook through mobile devices.

There is more. Approximately one out of every 8 people on earth is on Facebook and over half of the total users are logged in on any given day. Users above 35 years now make up 30% of users, while those aged 18 to 34 check their Facebook page once they wake up in the morning!

Many people find Facebook very useful for discovering and reconnecting with ex-schoolmates - even from primary school, extended families, and former work colleagues. The potential for networking, among other branding and promotional activities, on this medium alone is so huge: 16 million users in Nigeria, over 120 million in Africa! Think on this and begin to imagine the vast benefits awaiting you as you network on Facebook.

You can enjoy the socialising, but while you are at it, pay particular attention to your aim. You want to register your personality and keep yourself visible in the minds of people. This is an easily accessible market for your services and products. All you need to do is to open your mind to the possibilities out there and to follow the guidelines I will highlight soon.

Facebook has a wide range of applications for connecting with friends, business, and games. These tools make Facebook very interactive and effective for networking. The Status update is the most used feature. It allows you to keep your online associates up-to-date on your activities. You may also post short statements of wisdom or professional insight on a regular basis. Your aim here is to generate a continuous flow of conversation or interaction within your network of friends and with specific individuals when they post comments on your updates.

Users can upload an unlimited number of albums and photos. A user may tag other users in order to share her photos with them automatically. Use this feature as you would use a postcard. Your friends would appreciate your photos of special events, exotic places you visit, and even pets that you have.

The Facebook **Chat** facilitates instant messaging, which allows users to communicate with friends.

Marketplace is another fantastic, yet under-utilised feature on Facebook. Users can post free classified advertisements. All users in your network get to see the listings you post. It is a powerful tool to enhance your networking activities because it allows you to present your services and products to your online associates free of charge.

Facebook **Pages** are very effective for marketing. People are deleting whatever comes across directly as advertisements, but will respond to other interactive and dynamic presentations.

Facebook **Notes** is a blogging feature that allows tags and images. You can write a log and tag your friends thereby sharing it for their viewing.

Facebook may be a site for friends and acquaintances, but it is also a great platform for business networking, because of the massive, heterogeneous audience it commands. You would do well to explore and utilise the medium to your advantage.

LinkedIn.com

This is the social networking website where you present yourself as a professional. LinkedIn is the foremost professional networking website. It has over 450 million registered users worldwide, with 1 million of them being in Nigeria. Do you know that all the Fortune 500 companies are represented in LinkedIn? These are the biggest companies in the United States as ranked by their gross revenue. The biggest organisations in Nigeria are also represented here.

Statistics show that employees at director-level and above are very well represented on LinkedIn. It allows individuals and organisations to create profiles with corporate and professional information. It is a platform you should use to present your resume and professional profile. It is an opportunity to present you as a brand. Remember that millions of people and interested organisations will be able to access your profile.

Many people meet new people through online connections, and companies even post vacancies there. You are not an exception. It is time to step up your game. Many private individuals and small businesses in Nigeria use this platform to share information about their products, network with others, and to connect with buyers and clients.

There are so many things that LinkedIn can do for you, your career and your business. Let's look discuss some of them.

1. LinkedIn Will Position You as a Reputable Brand

LinkedIn will enhance your online accessibility and reputation. Nowadays, people Google your name to find out if you are an authentic person or represented online and to obtain other general information about you. Your LinkedIn profile will most often show up early in the hit list.

This is a good reason to sign up on LinkedIn and to maintain an updated professional profile. Another good thing about this is that LinkedIn provides links to your profiles on other websites such as links to personal websites.

2. LinkedIn Is Good for Business

You can prospect for new business relationships or opportunities using LinkedIn. A straightforward guide would be for you to get onto the website, register (if you do not have an account yet), and search for people, companies or groups you envisage as prospects.

The site also displays all information concerning your target and you can begin to initiate your connections from there. You can connect with people, join groups, and follow companies/organisations. If, for instance, you intend to do business with a company, you may begin your research about the company from here. You can also connect with the key players of the organisation with LinkedIn.

Another great thing about this is that you are also able to see the connections of your connections rated by degrees. A direct connection is a first-degree connection; a friend of your first-degree connection is a potential second-degree connection, and so on.

This reinforces the concept of compound networking, which we examined in chapter one. You can also initiate automatic referrals from your direct connections and you may begin to explore other networking possibilities from there.

3. LinkedIn Can Be Used for Talent Recruitment and Employment

LinkedIn is a prime avenue optimised with all the features to assist you in presenting yourself to prospective employers, offering hints, and advice. The website has powerful analytics that look at your profile and match you with suitable connections, organisations and individuals who may be in the position to get you that job.

Many international companies use LinkedIn as a tool for seeking out qualified candidates. It cuts their costs in talent recruitment campaigns because they can select prospective employees from suitable users with accessible profiles.

4.You Can Join Relevant Groups on LinkedIn

Many industry-specific or specialist groups also exist. The one many young Nigerians may like is tagged "Job openings, Job Leads and Job Connections!" These groups offer forums for collaboration and mentoring. You can even create one for yourself if you do not find any suiting your specific industry. People will join you in the course of time.

5. You Can Get Answers and Suggestions on Any Question and Topic with LinkedIn Answers

LinkedIn Answers provides an avenue for knowledge sharing on the website. Users can ask and answer questions. You can post questions to the entire LinkedIn network of users. You can use this forum to connect with users who answer your questions thereby building a network of experts and competent professionals required for your business or career growth. In the same vein, your answering questions will increase your credibility as an expert in your field.

Twitter

Twitter is a social website also known as a micro blogging website; because it allows users to post comments or status updates of not more than 140 characters. A tweet is a post or status update on Twitter. There are over 300 million registered users on Twitter. News spread fast you know. The viral nature of your message spreading can be used to make a difference; as well as initiate a business promotion campaign.

WhatsApp

According to the official website, more than 1 billion people in over 180 countries use WhatsApp to stay in touch with friends and family, anytime and anywhere. WhatsApp is free, and offers simple, secure, reliable messaging and calling. It is available on phones all over the world.

WhatsApp started as an alternative to SMS. The product now supports sending and receiving a variety of media like text, photos, videos, documents, and location, as well as voice calls. Messages and calls are secured with end-to-end encryption, meaning that no third party including WhatsApp can read or listen to them.

With WhatsApp Group Chat, you can keep in touch with the groups of people that matter the most, like your family or network. With group chats, you can also share messages, photos, and videos with up to 256 people at once. You can also name your group, mute or customize notifications, and more.

We have only mentioned a few of the available online platforms for business and social networking. There are so many others out there and many more are being developed everyday. Imagine the leverage this would give your business in terms of the huge clientele and referral base. When you factor in the concept of compounding relationships, the sky indeed can only be your starting point.

Cases in Point

Now, let me mention two actual scenarios to summarise the benefits of using these social services before I go on to blogging. The first is on collaboration. Collaboration has become the new competition these days. I want to affirm that you can be more productive, make more money, and build a stronger business just by maximising your online networking.

We have suitable forums to share our ideas, our needs, and resources with others across the globe. Perhaps the most popular and widely successful collaboration on the Internet is **Wikipedia**. Wikipedia is a free, web-multilingual encyclopedia project funded by donations from people all over the world. There are over 40 million articles written solely by volunteers. Its articles are cited to be as near accurate as that of Encyclopedia Britannica. The website remains a source of reliable information for users across every sector of life.

Another unique example is that of the critically acclaimed author, William Stallings, who utilised volunteers and contributors in his social networks to review his book before it was published.

I have discovered that it is possible for you to build a business from ground up by utilising the opportunities abounding on these social sites. Think about it: someone is out there who has some specialist knowledge or experience – or who knows some other person or group who could assist you in birthing the dream you have always held in your heart.

It is important to know that the things you need to succeed will begin to fall in line one after the other as you take the necessary steps in the right direction - chief among them is by connecting with the right people.

The Internet abounds with opportunities, and the resources there are so vast that sometimes we fear or actually experience information overload. Nevertheless, I enjoin you again with the words of Roosevelt: Start with what you have where you are.

Social scientists have explained a situation known as ambient awareness stating that regular usage of these social media enables people to become aware of one another's lives in a subconscious way. Online social media enable people and businesses to build closer bonds with their client base. The consumers and the brands become more personal, thereby fostering a relationship as a platform for increased patronage.

These days, your LinkedIn or Facebook accounts are not luxury items; rather, they add significant value to your brand. The rules of networking remain the same whether it is face-to-face or on the Internet - you must plan properly, you must come across as competent and authentic, and you must present a credible image. You need to keep in touch and be willing to give of yourself first before you begin to ask for referrals and business links. At the end of the day, it is not just about socialising but you are mindful of every opportunity to create a link between you and another person, and it could evolve into business sometime in the future.

Finally, a respectable online presence enhances your image as a professional in tune with the new social culture. You come across as credible, modern, and efficient. It is true that these tools became status symbols in themselves. Twenty years ago, an email address and a mobile telephone distinguished a credible professional amidst the crowd. As new platforms emerge, we strongly encourage to get acquainted with them.

USING BLOGS FOR BUSINESS AND SOCIAL NETWORKING

A **web log** otherwise called a **blog** is a journal of expert or personal opinion on particular subject matter or reviews on life/social events. According to statistic.com: There are over 300 million blogs on the Internet today.

You can use a Blog as a great way to register yourself as a visible professional rendering expert opinion on the Internet. Everyone is shopping for information and resources to help them live healthier, work smarter, earn more and to enjoy life's riches. You would do well to position and present yourself as a competent and resourceful individual using blogs. The returns, I daresay, would overwhelm you in due course.

You may decide to register and begin to publish your thoughts on one of the numerous blog sites available. You can also create your own website and include a blog link on the website. This can position you as an expert in your field or as a creative and interesting person. You may begin to write interesting articles on the culture of your organisation, your job as a professional, or your business. Your goal is to make your brand visible and credible, as you communicate vital and helpful information to your network regularly.

If you write about your hobby, you would attract people with similar interest. If it is on societal issues, a simple link to your blog might be all you need to create a connection and maintain a great reputation with your industry peers or friends. You can begin to strategise on how to become a trusted source of useful information to the massive audience on the Internet.

There are many different types of blogs: from personal blogs to corporate and political blogs; to travel and fashion, and from the arts to religion and technology. Just name any issue of interest, and there is at least a blog for it! Blogging is the new self-publishing. The new self PR. Blogs are a unique way to register your presence and maintain your visibility online, while creating an opportunity for networking: people see your blog site, read your posts, articles, establish a relationship with you; and only good could emanate from there.

Your blogging preference pertaining to content and presentation depends on the type of business you do or the areas of your interest. It is pertinent to keep in mind the brand you are trying to enhance and the best means to pass your message across to your selected audience. For example, it may be appropriate for you as a banker to blog on the arts. It may win you connections to a wider circle of clientele.

Your blog may open up to you the inner circle of art lovers and enthusiasts who are mostly high net-worth people. Blogging about politics, however, may not be suitable because some of your contacts will definitely have different political persuasions from yours. There is no reason to work against yourself by creating this kind of conflict.

Many type of blogs exist. Text-based blogs are the most common. However, a blog could be based on video - called a vlog. A blog made up of photos is called a photo blog. Others may be made up of sketches, and links appropriately labeled link blogs and sketch blogs. Of course, you may decide to mix the media types featured on your blog in your bid to give your associates a rich experience whenever they visit the blog.

> I came across a fascinating story of a young woman who got employed while still at the university. A public relations firm that wanted to recruit people who were already familiar or commenting on the corporate clients, logged onto Twitter, saw a tweet from this lady about one such company, and that got them hooked. A Google search revealed she had a blog. The firm checked it out and decided she was a suitable candidate. All of these without her knowing that any recruiting was going on. They called her, had a chat with her and that was it. Launch Squad co-founder, Jason Throckmorton remarked, "She never would have found us unless we found her."

Here in Nigeria, a young man has established a much sought-after relationship with one of the nation's foremost human resource coaches and mentors when the gentleman read his note on the Nigeria of his dreams on Facebook. The coach invited him over for lunch. In the note inviting him, the coach told the young man that he was delighted at reading his prophesy of glory for the nation.

What relationship do you seek? Perhaps, I would suggest you begin to publish your thoughts today. Who knows, you just might attract the people you have been chasing all the while.

In a sad reversal of the two cases I mentioned above, an employee of a company was once fired after just ten days of employment for discussing corporate secrets on his personal blog. The company's management ensured he removed the offending material before terminating his employment.

I would like to conclude this section by stating the Blogger's code of conduct as proposed by a group of stakeholders. It consists of seven ideas:

I. Take responsibility not just for your own posts, but also for the comments you allow on your blog.

2. Label your tolerance level for abusive comments. Let people know the consequences of posting abusive comments on your page. The consequences might including deleting the offending post or comment, blocking the offender from having access to your page or even reporting the person to law enforcement agencies.

3. Consider eliminating anonymous comments. Insist that people fully identify themselves when the post comments on your page.

4. Ignore the trolls. (A troll is one who posts inflammatory, extraneous, or off-topic messages in an online community.)

5. Take the conversation offline, and talk directly to your online contacts or friends. What we are saying here is that you should deepen the online relationship by calling people or even meeting them face-to-face. You can also look for an intermediary to help you with establishing the face-to-face connection with your online friends or contacts..

6. If you know someone who is behaving badly, tell him/her so.

7. Do not say anything online that you would not say in person or face to face.

The quality of your blog's content and your consistency will help you to achieve your aim. Readers and visitors will come to appreciate and respect you thereby building your credibility. You should also pay good attention to the layout of your blog, the text font, and the quality of the images, video, and audio that you use.

Make a habit of referring clients or prospective associates to your blog. Invite them to access information you feel they may be interested in. You should place links to direct people to your blog on other social platforms, or whenever you post a comment on other people's blogs.

RULES FOR NETWORKING ONLINE

The rules of business and social networking, whether physical or online are basically the same; and perhaps a little more. Some of the rules include:

1. Find a Common Ground

It could be shared work, industry, related hobby, same locality, religious belief or political persuasion. Just find a common ground that will serve as the fulcrum of your initiating a discussion with your prospect. It is important more than ever to establish a visible common ground upfront so there can be a basis for your target to accept you.

2. Connect

Introduce yourself, send an email, post a comment, send an inbox message or a professional invitation: For instance, "Hello Damilola, my name is John. I just saw your profile and I realise we are in the same industry. I will like to add you to my network. Hope we can collaborate on a worthwhile project in the future. Look forward to your response. Thank you." That's how to connect.

3. Add Value

You have to prove yourself useful to people. It is one thing to remain visible; it is another thing to be valuable. Aspire to be known as a reliable link and a provider of resources. When you come across any information or materials that might benefit your network, ensure you forward it to them. You can position yourself as a repository of resources, and people will begin to come to you for assistance.

Be the one to send an informative link, an eBook or an e-zine - whatever you see that would be of benefit to your connections. Even when you cannot be of help at a time, you would still come across as someone who cares. As the saying goes, "Touch a heart before you ask for a hand."

4. Use Recommendations and Referrals

Statistics show that 78% of consumers trust peer recommendations. On LinkedIn, you can ask your connections to endorse your work. The recommendations are placed in your profile and can make all the difference. The result can be enhanced reputation and credibility. It can also be a new business, a new contract, or a new job.

People generally rely on information from other people when making a choice; and in the online world, word of mouth rules! If I like it, I push it. And the 'IT' could be a product or service. Facebook's like button is perhaps one of the most endearing tools on the Internet.

You can create a public profile or group and leverage on recommendations from your friends and friend's friends. Remember that in networking your goal is to register your identity as well as what you have to offer in the minds of people. Utilize this same tool. Recommend people, products, and services. This is a guaranteed way to nurture your connections.

5. Stay in Touch

Comment on your friends' posts and updates. Find every opportunity to stay in touch. Watch out for birthdays, weddings, anniversaries, promotions, and change of jobs. Use every opportunity to celebrate and cheer your network connections/associates. Do all these without appearing desperate or overbearing.

6. Be Consistent

Update your profile and web pages regularly. An up-to-date profile or blog shows that you are concerned about your public image. It also helps to keep you visible in the minds of the people in your network.

7. Solidify Your Relationships

People are still more comfortable with meeting potential business partners or service providers face to face. The Internet and social sites are only tools. In the years ahead, we may become comfortable with virtual friends. Someone might say, "Meet my friend Julius. We've been online friends and business partners for the past 15 years."

While social sites and the Internet may allow you to initiate relationships with people and maintain such from the convenience of your mobile phone, you should make an effort to meet them physically. If you can, set up an appointment for you to meet physically.

It is imperative at this point that we also touch on the risks of networking online.

Due to its virtual nature, there are certain risks associated with online networking. The Privacy and security issues to be careful about may include:

1. **Anonymous Users**: It may be difficult for you to identify a person, or prove the identity of a person you are connecting with online. The worries include: "Who am I communicating with?" "How can I verify you are who you say you are?"

2. **Aggression and Abuse**: Occasionally, some people display irrational, aggressive behaviour on the Internet. Covert aggression, abuse, and exposure to unsolicited content; prominent among which is pornography, abound.

3. **Non-confidentiality of Information**: How does one certify that the information given out online remains confidential? This is perhaps the most important security concern for online networkers. Millions of people, including competitors, opponents, and criminally minded people may have access to the information you share online.

> **WARNING**
>
> Therefore, exercise some discretion when networking online. Do not disclose your personal information all at once. Do check the security status of websites you are networking. There are phishing websites impersonating authentic websites that receive and store the unsuspecting users' input. Criminals and hackers may use such information to carry out various cybercrime activities.

GUIDELINES AND STEPS FOR NETWORKING VIA THE SOCIAL MEDIA PLATFORMS

1. Be Discreet

Be careful about posting your ongoing activity or whereabouts on social sites. It is highly important for you to exercise some care with the amount of information and details you actually upload on social networking websites.

Robberies and murders have occurred because someone left too much information online. You should avoid posting personal information as much as possible.

If possible, avoid using your real names on such sites. Explore the privacy settings on social websites to determine who can view information in your profile or certain changes in your status.

> One morning an employee called in sick. Unfortunately, that same day she posted on Facebook pictures and updates of her having a great time with her partner at the beach! The boss saw the update and she returned the following day to be fired!

2. Do Not Respond to Everything:

Do not respond to every new application request on sites like Facebook. Unscrupulous individuals create seemingly fun applications requesting you to fill in some information so you would be able to view or use. Never fill in your full date of birth, names of parents and address details carelessly.

3. Be Sensitive

Identify the nature of the online medium you are using and tailor your language or expressions appropriately. For example, the kind of language you would use on Facebook and sound very authentic, might write you off totally on a site like LinkedIn. On Facebook, it may be all right to post: "Men, TGIF! Na where I go hang out tonight o? (Where am I hanging out tonight?)" Imagine that post on a prime, professional platform like LinkedIn. You would come across as silly, to say the least. Be sure to maintain a respectable front and take care not to offend people's sensibilities by your posts and comments.

18. Mind Your Grammar

You must use proper grammar when networking online. The text is the most prevalent means you are going to use to socialize and communicate with people. Try to avoid slangs and text-speak. Never use foul language or sensitive slangs on your platform. Express your information in simple terms; leave nothing for the imagination of the viewer or user to resolve.

In physical networking, it is easier to observe body language, tone of voice, facial expression, and other non-verbal cues of the person you are interacting with. However, most of the communication online is text-based. You would have to put in more effort to understand or be understood by the person you are connecting with. Learn to express yourself appropriately.

5. Be Honest

It is important to come across as an authentic person. Write what you know as you know it. In audio-visual situations, make sure your environment is clean and uncluttered. Eliminate background noise or debris. Be honest, be real. Remember, the folks out there can only see so much of you. Do not exaggerate.

19.   Avoid Derogatory Comments

A man posted defamatory comments about a Nigerian state governor. He abused him in so many graphic words; garnering quite a following. The governor responded by arresting and keeping him in police custody for days. He finally ended up in the court.

The things you say or do will either draw or repel people. You would want people to be drawn to you and for the right reasons too. Do not be tempted to go for notoriety unless you weigh it thoroughly and decide it will work to your advantage. That will work against most people.

7. Post Your Picture

Remember to change the default avatar or the default blank image the site uses to represent your picture. Do upload a picture that helps to project your desired image. Do not put up a picture of you at a party or with your face painted in a clown mask unless you are certain it will help your image. A clear headshot or passport photograph will be appropriate.

8. Be Complete

Fill your online profile completely so that people can know who you really are. You should however be mindful of your personal security; especially on general social websites like Facebook. Make sure you fill in your past employers, education, affiliations, and activities to further improve your chances of networking. Connecting with former colleagues and schoolmates will become more probable; members of professional organisations and people with similar hobbies and interests will also be able to connect with you.

Networking is all about positioning you to achieve success, and no better platform exists in today's world than through the Internet. Alex Haley, the author of the classic, Roots, said, "If you see a turtle on a fence post, know that he must have had some help getting there."

That is what networking does for us. There are opportunities waiting for you out there. Seize the moment!

ON MARBLE

"When we're together or when we're apart, you're first in my thoughts and first in my heart".
– Author Unknown

Action Plans

Action Plans